delicious days

Nicole Stich

delicious days

GIFT FROM THE
Cahill's
PURE

Contents

Truth is, I'm always hungry. I quite positively think about eating more than three times a day. Consequently triggering the idea of writing about cooking. And as a result, people have been reading my thoughts on it and the recipes that have become dear to me in my food blog deliciousdays.com. It was distinguished by Time Magazine—as one of the 50 coolest websites in the world. And turned my life upside down! Yet one thing hasn't changed: My favorite pastime is still thinking about what I could conjure up next in my kitchen.

Nicky

Reisshauer

THE GIRL WHO SET OUT TO LEARN ABOUT ENJOYMENT

If someone had predicted to my parents that I would one day write a cookbook, they probably would have been spared some sleepless nights. I was what most people would call spoiled– at least when it came to eating. No herbs in the soup, no onions in the vegetables, and mushrooms only when they couldn't be recognized as such. The list was endless. Children can be very imaginative when it comes to reasons for why they don't want to eat something, and that especially applied to me.

This only changed when I began to spend the weekends with my grandparents. Almost everything revolved around food at their place. The heavily laden trees in the orchard were waiting to be harvested, the cucumbers and zucchini in the greenhouse twined out of control, and the bread came from my uncle's little village bakery where my grandmother helped out on most days. She had a masterful understanding of how to include me and my friends in the kitchen and in the garden, even when we–equipped with rubber boots and the hose–liked to flood the beds, impatiently snitched radishes that were much too small, or picked the green heirloom apples from the branches. My grandmother's culinary skills were obviously one of the reasons why I liked to visit her so much. Her down-to-earth cooking regularly enticed the entire family to gather around the table. Even as a small child, I admired the devotion with which she stood behind the stove every day and fed her family time and again in addition to her job as a seamstress and teacher.

Unfortunately, my beloved grandmother passed away much too young–and along with her many of her traditional family recipes since she had recorded very few of them in written form. I had left home in the meantime to go to college and made my first attempts in my own teeny-weeny student kitchen. My parents had given me the refrigerator and the stove was a relic from my great-grandmother's apartment, but it was certainly adequate for what I had in mind: duplicating my granny's cherished dishes–even if I didn't have the written recipes. It was an advantage that I had watched and helped her cook and bake for years, so I was already familiar with the individual steps. The rest was persevering trial-and-error. And so I discovered in passing how much I actually enjoy the work in the kitchen.

I began to cook for good friends on a regular basis. At that time–Jamie Oliver was still unknown and cooking was anything but hip–I was initially rewarded with well-meant jibes: I would definitely make a great housewife, just in case my education didn't work out... And despite this, everyone liked to gather around my dining table over and over again.

> "delicious days is pure elegance. A knock-out beauty of a site. Of course I appreciate the focus on seasonal, local ingredients and classical cooking methods. But Nicky and Oliver take it a step further. They bring an artist's attention to detail and grace as they present their kitchen adventures. Each post is a little jewel, reflecting an inspired vision of what home cooking can be."
>
> **Elise Bauer, Carmichael**
> **www.simplyrecipes.com**

Although I succeeded in duplicating almost all of my grandmother's favorite recipes years later, I also realized that there were many exciting things to discover in other countries and cuisines. It is still a tremendous joy for me to invite dear friends to my table and cook for them. Because: I believe that cooking and good food are the easiest way to make someone happy.

GOING OFFLINE—FROM BLOG TO BOOK

While searching for a recipe online, I came across food blogs in early 2005 and was instantly fascinated. People around the world write about their culinary experiences and their favorite recipes on these websites—in a way that is sometimes more, sometimes less personal, exchange tips and opinions, or discuss the latest trends in the kitchen. A handful of blogs quickly became part of my daily reading routine because I was inspired by the enthusiasm with which the food bloggers dedicated themselves to their favorite topic. So I obviously played with the thought of writing my own blog a short time later. Countless ideas were born and rejected just as quickly. I looked for an appropriate name, and my boyfriend Oliver helped me with the technical implementation in the following days: It was finally ready on March 6, 2005. I clicked the "upload" button one last time and my little blog www.deliciousdays.com was born. Did I know what I was getting myself into?

"The sublime photos draw you in. The recipes inform and inspire. And the icing on the cake is a dose of humor stirred into the mix. I've been a loyal reader of delicious days since I first landed on the site years ago, and since then, delicious days remains at the top of my favorite food blogs. It's everything a food blog should be: classy, personal, mouth-watering, but it's not just food porn. The writing style is playful and engaging. It's abundantly clear that Nicky is having a lot of fun in the kitchen. I join the legions of fans who are awaiting what is sure to be a fabulous book"

David Lebovitz, Paris
www.davidlebovitz.com

The first articles, mostly recipes with a little personal story, went online. And while the question as to whether anyone would even read them still popped into my head, the first feedback was already making its way in—I had apparently hit a nerve with my little recipe anecdotes and blog design. But the biggest challenge was the accompanying recipe pictures. Anyone who has ever tried to entice an appealing photo of a serving of homemade spaghetti on the home kitchen table from a little digicam may have an idea of how frustrating my first attempts were (too dark, blurry, is that dog food?).

But the few good pictures that were probably created by chance at the beginning were enough to awaken my ambition. I began to get involved in food photography and quickly noticed that the impeccably styled dishes in slick magazines were not what really appealed to me. I preferred the enticing, authentic pictures in daylight that were still mouth-watering and perhaps also revealed a new perspective or focused on an unusual detail. It certainly took a bit of practice and, above all, time at the beginning to put every dish on the table in an appetizingly prepared way without any aids or tricks and capture it in an appealing photo. However, this ensured that my readers would get a photo of the recipe that was realistically doable—what you see is what you get. When trying to prepare a recipe due to the promising photos, I had already been frustrated too many times because the results on my plate unfortunately had nothing at all in common with the artistically styled picture.

The next gift to myself was a small, digital reflex camera with a tripod—and I still work with both today. Since the cooking, arranging, and photographing always takes place in our kitchen, a state of emergency sometimes prevails there. Pots and plates are piled up next to the recipe texts and the spare silverware while part of the food is still simmering on the stove. There are often just a few

minutes in which a dish can be photographed in a fresh and optically appealing way without aids—it's certainly easier to succeed in this with a panna cotta than a scoop of melting sorbet. Another factor is obviously also my rumbling stomach that usually can hardly wait for the food to fulfill its true purpose...

The way I write recipes has also changed because of the blog. Designed for the quickest possible contact by means of comments or e-mail, blog authors get immediate feedback from their readers—both positive and negative. Errors or discrepancies are swiftly discovered. Even though my recipes have been formulated quite precisely, I very much encourage everyone to adapt them to their own taste. I believe that a recipe is just an inspiration and rough guide, upon which you can put your own very personal stamp with increasing experience and intuition. Another factor involved is that local circumstances such as taste, quality, and availability of the food, humidity, or elevation play an essential role and cannot be generalized (also see page 208 on this topic).

I'm surprised over and over again by how enthusiastically people respond to recipes, especially when they are associated with their own memories. A certain taste, or an aroma wafting from the oven, can take you back for a fraction of a second to a long-forgotten moment. My grandmother's traditional recipes are the best example of this. If I can help someone to experience such a little moment of happiness or a reader writes that my cake recipe has turned her into the most popular colleague in the office, then this is the most beautiful aspect of food blogging for me—apart from the many lovely people that I have met as a result of it.

All the same, I was still initially flabbergasted when a publishing company contacted me and suggested that we produce a book together. Even though I certainly read and collect cookbooks like other people collect novels and my blog had now accumulated a considerable number of readers, could I really write my own cookbook? I brooded over it and pondered about how I would present my own book until I got a call from an editor of the Gräfe und Unzer publishing house. They not only wanted to start a book project with me, but also thought it was very important for me to realize my own ideas and give the book my own signature. That was the decisive factor for me.

A good year has now passed and the idea actually turned into a book, which I hope will inspire people, whet their appetites, and find a place both in the kitchen and on the sofa. It would make me happy if you read delicious days with just as much enjoyment as I had in writing it.

“I am always stunned by Nicky and Oliver's ingenuity and what they have done with their creation, Delicious Days. The amount of care and labor that they have put into this handcrafted site, from the luscious photography to the beautiful design (not to mention the wonderful cooking), never ceases to amaze me. Nicky's writing sings with the joy of culinary discovery—whether it's a fantastic recipe she can't wait to share, a novel technique, or curiosity and excitement about a new ingredient. And, when she faces the rare culinary challenge (as most home cooks inevitably do) she tells it like it is, with her trademark wit and humor. Countless readers around the world, many of whom are food bloggers themselves, are addicted to Nicky's stories of her latest food finds, discoveries, and travels. Delicious Days has all of the best qualities of what a blog can do—Nicky has opened up her world to ours, and we are reaping the benefits. Who knew that there was so much delicious cooking going on in Munich!”

Josh Friedland, New York
www.thefoodsection.com

I REALLY JUST WANTED SOMETHING TO EAT

Did I buy the right organic brand? Why do my soups always taste so bland? Did my lemon chicken really have a happy life and am I totally out of touch if I have no idea of what to do with melon caviar? A bit of food for thought and tips related to cooking and enjoying, why our own kitchen ego needs care, and why the wrong attitude is guaranteed to stand in the way...

Kitchen karma: It's completely okay to have a bit of dread and respect when it comes to culinary challenges. But you are not doing yourself a favor if you like to tell yourself that the caramel is certain to burn again and the yeast dough is sure not to rise. A bit of trust in your own abilities and a different recipe can often work true wonders!

Everything tastes twice as good in a circle of friends. Even if you are still at the start of your kitchen career, you should gather friends and family around the table for feasting on a regular basis and create your own traditions. The motto is "less is more"–one single good dish delights guests more than a distraught host with a bungled 5-course menu.

> "delicious days…what can I say. Nicky's creations are seriously addictive and all very approachable at the same time—best of all, the recipes are easy to follow and work every time. If you thought you'd never venture into making your own pasta or anything else that seems unobtainable from the home kitchen, delicious days will help bring out the three-star chef within you!"
>
> **Johanna Wagner, London**
> **www.thepassionatecook.com**

The salt in the soup: Even if a recipe is written in greatest detail, no one can do the seasoning and tasting for you. "Too much" is at least as bad as "too little" in this case. Tasting the dish several times before serving helps to develop a good sense of this and is rewarded with a well-rounded taste.

Trends & kitchen toys: Cooking has now been "in" again for the past few years. Almost every TV station has its own cooking shows, and the industry has also long discovered the target group of the hobby cooks. New trends are created and innovative types of kitchen helpers are marketed. But you really need very few gimmicks to cook well. Even in the smallest kitchen, you can perform true wonders at the stove if you do it with passion–and that's something that money really can't buy.

Yes to tolerance, no to dogmatism: When various cultural and culinary influences meet in the kitchen, the result can be exciting new creations, as long as you don't fight over the "only" true way to prepare food or the "best" eating habits.

Organic & co.: A meal is only as good as its ingredients, which is why you should select food according to its quality and its taste, but not its price–depending obviously on how much you can afford. Compare, try out, and take advantage of regional and seasonal offers in the process. Depend less on the labels than on your own judgment.

Your own style will develop completely on its own. By coupling self-confidence with experience. Being able to already taste a recipe on your tongue when just reading through it. Trying out new ideas of your own with curiosity and a gut instinct. And if something goes wrong once in a while: learn from your mistakes and laugh about them.

tiny & tasty

PITTOLE

During my student years in Regensburg, we often went to our favorite little Italian restaurant that had these golden-brown deep-fried dough pillows as antipasti on the menu—unfortunately, the chef never wanted to disclose his recipe. But he did give me one tip: The dough is very similar to normal pizza dough. After a few attempts, I got the hang of it and the little pittole tasted almost better than at the »Dolce Vita«!
Incidentally, the amount of garlic and rosemary can be adapted completely to your taste. But there is one thing that you really must keep in mind: Pittole are so popular that the main course will quickly become irrelevant.

MAKES ABOUT 50 PIECES
PREPARATION TIME: 45 MINUTES
PLUS 30–45 MINUTES RISING TIME

Yeast Dough
300 g/10.5 oz flour
(possibly a bit more)
1 tsp salt
20 g/0.75 oz fresh yeast
1 pinch sugar
2 tbsp olive oil

For Deep-Frying
3 cloves of garlic
3–5 rosemary sprigs
Olive oil

Place flour and salt in a large bowl and mix. Make a well in the center. Crumble the yeast into a small bowl. Add 200 ml/7 fl oz lukewarm water and the sugar, then stir and pour into the well. Add 1 tbsp olive oil and knead everything by hand or with an electric mixer. The dough must be smooth and hardly sticky. If not, add flour by the tablespoon until it reaches the desired consistency. Sprinkle the dough with flour, cover, and let rise in a warm place for 30–45 minutes. It should approximately double the volume.

Peel the garlic, rinse the rosemary and pat it dry. Combine both in a largish pan or a wok and cover with about two inches of olive oil. The pieces of dough should be able to float freely. Heat the oil (maximum 180°C/355°F). Briefly knead the dough again in the meantime. Lightly sprinkle the work surface with flour and roll out the dough until it is about 2.5 cm/1 inch thick. Cut into small squares (each side about 4 cm/1.5 inches in length).

Then deep-fry a test piece: If the oil bubbles and the piece of dough rises, then the oil is hot enough. But it should definitely not start to smoke! Put the dough squares into the oil one by one and turn them several times to bake until golden brown. Then place on kitchen paper and let excess fat drain.

Serve the warm pittole with smoked ham, cheese, and antipasti.

GOAT CHEESE WITH GREEN NUT DRESSING

I inherited a peculiar culinary taste from my dear mom: Both of us often prefer a good dressing to the salad around it. I still clearly remember the constant indignation at my grandparents' dining table when both of us tried to be as inconspicuous as possible while spooning the last drops of Grandma Luise's dressing for the endive salad out of our salad bowls—or totally brazen—even slurping it up. Wasn't that a big compliment for the cook? I still catch myself doing this occasionally today, but that must be acceptable within my own four walls...

The olive oil and the chopped pistachios give this dressing its remarkable green-yellow color. A mild honey together with the white wine vinegar harmonizes wonderfully with the fruit in the salad. That's how good a favorite dressing tastes!

ENOUGH FOR 4 AS A SMALL APPETIZER AND FOR 2 AS A SALAD
PREPARATION TIME: 30 MINUTES

Dressing

8–10 shelled walnut halves
1 heaping tbsp unsalted shelled pistachios
6 tbsp fruity olive oil
2 tbsp mild honey
1 tbsp white wine vinegar
1 pinch salt

Salad

1/2 head frisée salad
1 small Belgian endive
1 large, slightly tart apple
1 large pear
1 handful of black grapes
100 g/3.5 oz mature soft goat cheese (log)

Preheat oven to 180°C/355°F (convection oven 160°C/320°F). Turn on grill (if there is one).

Prepare the dressing first: Use a knife or electric processor to grind walnuts and pistachios into a relatively fine mixture. Combine in a bowl with the rest of the dressing ingredients.

Then clean the lettuce. Tear the frisée into small, bite-sized pieces and cut the Belgian endive into very thin stripes. Briefly wash the lettuce and spin dry. Wash the apple and pear well (both are used with the peel), cut into quarters, and remove the cores. Cut the fruit quarters into thin pieces. Wash and halve the grapes. Arrange the apple, pear, and grapes together with the lettuce in small bowls.

Cut the goat cheese into thin pieces and place on a baking sheet covered with parchment paper. Bake until golden brown in oven, as close as possible to the grill coils (since this happens in just a few minutes, be sure to stay nearby so the cheese doesn't burn). Carefully arrange with a spatula on the prepared salad and sprinkle with the dressing before serving.

STUFFED MEDJOOLS WITH BACON

On the way to the Farmers Market at Ferry Plaza in San Francisco, Sherry asked us if we were familiar with the Californian Medjool dates. No? Well, then we absolutely had to try them—and changed the menu planning for dinner that night right then and there. We leisurely strolled from one market stall to the next, absolutely enraptured by the delicacies offered for sampling at the individual stands. Because we were allowed to try little morsels everywhere we went, it took us quite a while to work our way through the entire shopping list. The stall owners raved about their products with such enthusiasm that we obviously bought much more in the end than we had actually planned.

"Here, try one of these!" Sherry held the bag with the dates she had just bought under our noses. The sun-dried Medjools even looked different from regular dates because of their slightly wrinkled skin with its almost bluish shimmer. But their true potential developed at the first bite: The creamy flesh reminded us of the sweetest caramel and chestnuts, explaining why this variety is called the "Queen of Dates". They are true energy boosters, make an outstanding snack now and then, and give an Oriental touch to salads and desserts. That very evening, Sherry served them to us filled with smoked almonds. When we returned home, I was thrilled to discover that even our vegetable grocer around the corner occasionally offers Medjool dates from California. Be sure to try them!

FOR 4 AS AN APPETIZER
PREPARATION TIME: 30 MINUTES

16 Medjool dates
100 g/3.5 oz soft goat cheese or Gorgonzola dolce
16 thin strips of bacon (you can use regular breakfast bacon, but Italian Pancetta or Coppa—and especially Lardo—bacon has a spicier flavor)

Plus
16 toothpicks

Cut the dates lengthwise with a small, sharp knife and carefully squeeze out the seeds (the dates should stay as intact as possible). Fill each of them with just enough goat cheese (I like to use a mild variety) so that the dates can be closed completely. Then tightly wrap each piece with 1 slice of bacon and secure with a toothpick.

Set the dates on a cookie sheet lined with parchment paper and bake in the oven preheated to 200°C/390°F (convection oven 180°C/355°F) on the middle rack for 10–15 minutes. Or place the Medjools in a pan (without adding any fat) and sauté over medium heat on all sides until crisp in 3–5 minutes.

There are endless possibilities for varying this recipe: The goat cheese or Gorgonzola can be replaced by other types of cheese (such as Pecorino or Manchego), but lightly roasted almonds or walnuts also make an excellent filling.

OVEN-DRIED TOMATOES

I still have a good memory of how the first dried tomatoes appeared in the delis and at the antipasti counters and how quickly they became essential for anyone who wanted to give their dishes a touch of Mediterranean flair. Whether stewed along with beef roulades, finely chopped in pasta dishes, or as the standard in every tramezzini—they were simply everywhere. Unfortunately, many of the representatives of their kind are just a sad imitation of how they are supposed to be—tough, dry, and often quite overpowering in taste. But you can come up with results that are a thousand times better at home in your own oven. All you need is a little patience. Every variety of tomato is basically suitable for slow drying in the oven. My own favorites are the small cherry tomatoes that you can actually get year round in good quality. If I want to prepare these tomatoes for guests, I like to plan their preparation so that they come out of the oven just before the guests arrive—then they only need to follow this wonderful aroma to find the way to their kitchen. Serve the tomatoes on their own, in pasta, or with buffalo mozzarella.

MAKES 1 COOKIE SHEET FULL OF CHERRY TOMATOES
PREPARATION TIME: 15 MINUTES PLUS 4–6 HOURS OF DRYING TIME

500 g/1.1 lb cherry tomatoes (or other varieties of tomatoes)
Olive oil for the cookie sheet

To taste
Coarse sea salt
Finely minced garlic
Fresh small thyme leaves

Preheat oven to 90°C/195°F (convection oven not recommended). Wash the cherry tomatoes, pat dry, and cut in half. Regular tomatoes can obviously also be dried in the oven by removing the stalk after washing and before cutting them into quarters or sixths, depending on the size. Some recipes recommend also removing the seeds together with the juice—but this results in the tomatoes quickly becoming too dry for my taste.

Spread a fair amount of oil olive on a cookie sheet (or a large ovenproof dish) and distribute the tomato halves on it with the cut side up. Sprinkle with sea salt, garlic, and thyme according to taste, but not too generously because the flavors become even more intense during the slow oven-drying process.

Put the sheet (or dish) on the middle rack in the oven and let the tomatoes dry for 4–6 hours, depending on their size. Be sure to check on them once in a while since the overall time can vary quite a bit depending on the size of the tomatoes used and the desired degree of dryness. But this is also a good excuse for trying them every now and then!

Take the tomatoes out of the oven as soon as they have reached the desired consistency and serve. They can also be kept in the refrigerator for a few days. It's best to use a container with a lid for this purpose and cover them with the best olive oil (which also takes on a fruity tomato aroma that goes well with bruschetta or a caprese salad).

BAGUETTE WITH LEMON-PARMESAN BUTTER

A warm, wonderfully crisp baguette with homemade herb butter, fresh from the oven (including greasy fingers)—some things just can't be improved. But my variation is at least a serious competitor: Although the lemon-parmesan butter may not look any different than herb butter, the fresh citrus taste and the chili spiciness give it a decent kick.

ENOUGH FOR 1 BAGUETTE
PREPARATION TIME: 30 MINUTES
PLUS 5–15 MINUTES FOR BAKING

Spread

1/2–1 large green chili pepper
1 shallot
1 clove of garlic (optional)
1/2 small bunch of chives
125 g/4.5 oz soft butter
2 tbsp olive oil
1 organic lemon
1 organic lime
40 g/1.5 oz freshly grated Parmesan
Sea salt
Freshly ground black pepper

Base

1 baguette

Wash the chili pepper, remove the stalk and seeds. Peel the shallot and garlic (optional). Wash the chives and shake dry. Chop everything very fine and place in a bowl with butter and olive oil. Mix with a fork.

Wash the lemon and lime under hot water, then finely grate the zest (without the bitter white pith), and stir into the butter with the Parmesan. Carefully season to taste with salt and pepper because the Parmesan already gives it quite a bit of seasoning.

If you don't use the lemon-parmesan butter right away, you can keep it in the refrigerator—preferably in an airtight container. Or shape it into a roll and wrap firmly in plastic wrap.

You can then prepare a lemon-parmesan-butter baguette with this in two different ways:

1. Crisp variation: Preheat the oven to 180°C/355°F (convection oven 160°C/320°F) and also turn on the grill. Cut the baguette into slices, generously spread with the soft butter, and place on a baking sheet. Bake until golden brown and crisp on the highest rack in the oven, but don't let them get too dark. This takes about 5 minutes.

2. Soft and juicy variation: Preheat the oven to 200°C/390°F (convection oven 180°C/355°F). Slash the baguette in even intervals, as if you wanted to cut it into slices, but don't completely separate them. Generously spread the soft butter between the individual slices and distribute any remaining amounts on the bread crust. Wrap in aluminum foil and bake for 15 minutes on the middle rack.

BOQUERONES EN VINAGRETA

When you walk into a tapas bar in Spain for the first time, you may wonder about all the trash lying around on the floor. But this is a good sign: people eat good food here and lots of it—throwing the napkins & co. on the floor afterward has a long tradition. We discovered the best boquerones in such a tapas bar in Barcelona and quickly made the decision to also try the recipe on our own. If you don't shy away from taking the time to gut the small fish, you will be rewarded with an authentic tapa that is best enjoyed on its own with some white bread.

ENOUGH FOR 6 AS APPETIZER
PREPARATION TIME: 45 MINUTES
PLUS 30 MINUTES FOR MACERATING
PLUS 24 HOURS FOR MARINATING

500 g/1.1 lb anchovies
1 lemon
5 tbsp sherry vinegar
5–6 cloves of garlic
1 large red chili pepper
5 sprigs of parsley
Coarse sea salt
Freshly ground black pepper
Olive oil for covering

Wash anchovies under cold running water and gut them: Pinch off the heads with your index finger and thumb while pulling out the guts at the same time. Scratch the belly side with the help of your thumbnail. Completely open the belly, remove the center bones, and take off the tail. This will give you two fillets. Wash them carefully under cold running water before letting them briefly dry on paper towels.

Layer fillets in a bowl. Squeeze the juice of the lemon and sprinkle it evenly together with the vinegar. Let macerate for about 30 minutes. This will change the appearance of the anchovies, turning their slightly pink-colored flesh to white. Then rinse the fillets one last time and leave to drain on paper towels.

Peel the cloves of garlic. Wash the chili pepper and remove the stalk. Rinse off the parsley and shake dry. Chop everything finely and layer in a flat bowl or ovenproof dish alternately with the anchovy filets. Always put a little salt and pepper on top. Finally, pour in enough olive oil so that all of the fillets are covered. Let marinate in a container with a lid for 24 hours in the refrigerator.

MINI-QUICHES

Quiches are among my favorite contributions to any picnic or brunch with friends. After all, they are easy to transport and have many different possibilities for variations. Mini-quiches are even better because plates and knives are unnecessary for this perfect finger-food. I usually don't stick to any specific recipe for them, but just raid my supplies: a bit of bacon, a finely chopped vegetable, fresh herbs, the rest of a piece of cheese. You can always bake something delicious out of these and, thanks to the store-bought puff pastry, they don't take too much effort either. But now that my friends almost always extend an invitation in the same breath with "could you maybe bring the small quiches with apple and bacon?", I have included this recipe in my permanent repertoire.

MAKES 12 MINI-QUICHES
PREPARATION TIME: 25 MINUTES
PLUS 20 MINUTES FOR BAKING

2 red onions
8 slices of Pancetta
1 large, tart apple
3–4 thyme sprigs
3 tbsp butter
Freshly ground black pepper
1 large egg
100 g/3.5 oz cream
100 g/3.5 oz sour cream or crème fraîche
Salt
Freshly ground nutmeg
1 sheet of puff pastry (about 25 x 40 cm/10x16 inches from the refrigerated section)
About 100 g/3.5 oz Gorgonzola Dolce

Plus

12-cup muffin tin
Stripes of parchment paper, about 1 cm/0.5 inch thick

Peel, halve, and cut onions into fine strips. Do the same with the Pancetta. Quarter, peel, and core the apple. Then cut into very fine slices. Rinse thyme, shake dry, and pluck off the little leaves. Melt 2 tbsp butter in a pan. Brown Pancetta, onions, and apple over medium heat until the onions are glossy. Season with pepper and about half the thyme, then remove from the stove. Mix the egg with cream and sour cream or crème fraîche in a bowl, then season with salt, pepper, and nutmeg.

Preheat oven to 180°C/355°F (convection oven 160°C/320°F). Grease a muffin tin with the rest of the butter. To remove the quiches more easily from the pan after baking, also add a strip of parchment paper to each of the cups.

With a round pastry cutter or a glass, roll out and cut 12 circles (about 9 cm/3.5 inches Ø) of puff pastry. Shape into little bowls with your fingers and place into the cups of the muffin tin. Evenly spread the onion mixture over the puff pastry and top each with a little piece of Gorgonzola. Use a tablespoon to add the egg-cream, but just fill to 1 cm/0.5 inch below the top so that they don't spill in the oven when they rise. Use the rest of the thyme to garnish and bake until golden brown on the middle rack in the oven for about 20 minutes. Take out of the oven, let cool for 5 minutes, and carefully remove from the tin. They taste good either warm or cold.

HOT WONTONS WITH PLUM DIP

It takes a little practice to shape these wontons without damaging their thin cover, but it's worth the effort. Be careful, don't underestimate these tasty little tidbits—they are hot! If you would like them to be not quite as spicy, just reduce the amount of chili and ginger to accommodate your taste buds.

MAKES 30 WONTONS
PREPARATION TIME: 1 HOUR
PLUS 1 HOUR FOR MARINATING

Plum Dip

1 piece of fresh ginger (about 3 cm/ 1.25 inch)
1 garlic clove
1/4–1/2 large red chili pepper
6 large purple plums
2–3 tbsp sherry vinegar
4 tbsp brown sugar
1 pinch of salt

Wontons

1 piece of fresh ginger (about 5 cm/ 2 inches)
2 garlic cloves
2 large red chili peppers
2 green onions (scallions)
400 g/14 oz beef steak (such as sirloin)
1 tsp salt
1 tbsp honey
2 tbsp sesame oil
3 tbsp oyster sauce
30 frozen wonton wrappers
(10x10 cm/4x4 inches, from the Asian store)
1 large egg white
Peanut oil for deep-frying

For the dip, peel the ginger and garlic, wash the chili and remove the stem, and mince all together. Quarter the plums, peel, and remove the pits, then cut into small pieces. Put everything into a pot together with the remaining ingredients and 100 ml/3.5 fl oz water. Simmer over medium heat. As soon as the plums are cooked soft (after 10–15 minutes), use a hand-held blender to puree until smooth. If the consistency of the dip is too thick, dilute with a little water and season to taste again. Then let it cool.

For the wontons, peel the ginger and garlic, then wash the chilies and remove the stems. Wash and clean the green onions, then cut away the green parts. Chop everything finely together—either by hand or in a food processor—and place in a bowl. Cut the meat into wafer-thin strips, place in the bowl, and mix everything well. Mix in the salt, honey, sesame oil, and oyster sauce. Cover the filling and let marinate for about 1 hour in the refrigerator.

In the meantime, thaw the wonton wrappers in a stack under a moist dishtowel (this is how to keep them soft without drying them out).

One by one, carefully strip away the individual wrappers from the stack. Brush the edges with the egg white and place some of the filling in the center. Now pinch together all four corners of the wrapper over the filling and carefully close with the fingers to form little sacks.

Pour at least 4 cm/2 inches of peanut oil into a pot or wok and heat to 180°C/355°F. (Dip a wooden spoon into the oil. If little air bubbles appear immediately, then the oil is hot enough.) Don't place too many wontons into the oil at one time. Deep-fry until golden brown by turning them a number of times. Let excess fat drain off onto a thick layer of paper towels. Serve with the plum dip.

MUSHROOM CROSTINI

This recipe has already accompanied me for more than 15 years, but it still outshines more elaborately prepared dishes on a regular basis. However, our long-lasting liaison was almost not meant to be. I prepared two entire sheets of them for a party that was much too big in my student apartment that was much too small and maneuvered them without much ado into the oven for a lack of storage surface. Unfortunately, this only occurred to me again when we were cleaning up that night. But the remaining hard-working helpers were happy about the unexpected snack and not a crumb was left over. By the way, the baguette tastes incomparably better if it is served fresh!

MAKES ABOUT 12 CROSTINI
PREPARATION TIME: 20–30 MINUTES

Topping

300 g/10.5 oz champignons or button mushrooms
1–2 tbsp butter or olive oil
2 tbsp marsala (optional)
2 tbsp cream
Freshly grated nutmeg
Sea salt
Freshly ground black pepper
2 limes or 1 lemon
Chives as garnish

Base

1 baguette
4 tbsp butter or olive oil

For the topping, clean the mushrooms with a damp towel or soft brush and cut off the ends of the stems. Cut the mushrooms into very thin slices. Heat butter or olive oil (depending on your taste) over medium heat in a pan and add the mushrooms. Stir occasionally. As soon as the mushrooms have shrunk—they lose much of their original volume— add the marsala and cream, then season to taste with the nutmeg, salt, and pepper. Simmer slightly until most of the liquid has boiled away (this just takes a few minutes).

In the meantime, squeeze out the lime or lemon juice. Wash the chives, shake dry, and cut into round thin slices. Cut the baguette into thumb-thick pieces. Heat the butter or olive oil in a pan and fry the bread slices on both sides over medium heat until golden brown and crispy, then remove from pan.

Immediately cover the baguette slices with plenty of hot mushrooms, sprinkle generously with citrus juice, and top with the pepper and chives. Serve while still warm.

CHEZ FIGARO
Diners Spectacles Musicales
des ITALIENS . PARIS

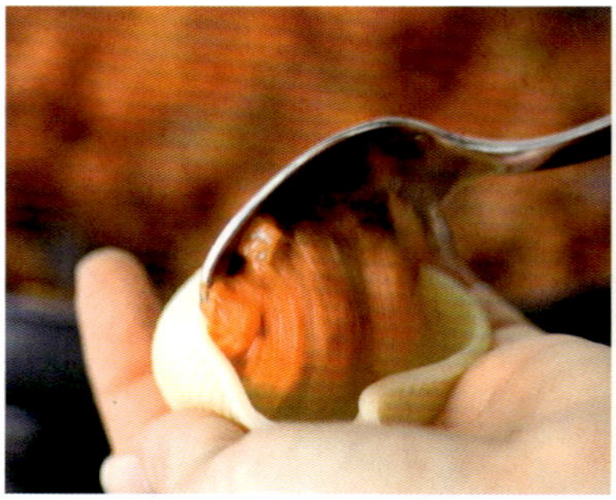

RATATOUILLE SHELLS AU GRATIN

When I discover a new kind of pasta while shopping, I am very rarely able to resist temptation. My pasta supply is thus pretty extensive. Having said that, very few varieties ultimately make it into my standard repertoire, which primarily consists of penne, casareccia, linguine, spaghetti, pappardelle, and orecchiette. But sometimes a spontaneously purchased kind of pasta opens up completely new possibilities, and this is what happened with these shells that are the size of a baby's fist. The inspiration for the filling was a coincidence because the ratatouille leftover from the previous day was awaiting its fate. But who could have guessed that this would turn into a friendship for life? Warm or cold, they are a pleasure au gratin with two kinds of Italian cheese.

SERVES 6–8 PERSONS AS APPETIZER
PREPARATION TIME: 45 MINUTES
PLUS 10–15 MINUTES FOR BAKING

250 g/9 oz conchiglie (noodles in shell form)
Salt
1 red onion
1 garlic clove
1 red chili pepper
1 eggplant
1 zucchini
1 yellow pepper
250 g/9 oz canned tomatoes
3–4 thyme sprigs
250 g/9 oz buffalo mozzarella
3 tbsp olive oil (plus a bit more for the form)
3 tbsp tomato paste
100 g/3.5 oz cream
Freshly grj26ound black pepper
1 pinch sugar
Medium hot, smoked paprika powder (Pimenton de la Vera)
100 g/3.5 oz mascarpone

For the pasta, boil plenty of salt water. Add the conchiglie and simmer according to package instructions until they are cooked but still firm to the bite (al dente). Then drain and rinse with cold water to prevent them from sticking together.

While the noodles cook, prepare the vegetables: Peel the onion and garlic, wash the chili and remove the stem, and then chop everything finely. Wash the eggplant, zucchini, and pepper. Clean and cut into small cubes. Coarsely chop the canned tomatoes. If necessary, remove the stems: Rinse the thyme, shake dry, and pluck off the little leaves. Cut the mozzarella into small cubes.

Heat a large pan, add the oil and briefly brown the onion, garlic, and chili pepper. Add the diced vegetables and lightly brown for about 10 minutes over medium heat. Stir in the tomato paste and briefly sauté it together with the other ingredients. Then add the tomatoes and pour in the cream. Season with salt and pepper, sugar, paprika powder, and thyme. Then let simmer for another 5 minutes over low heat. Remove the ratatouille vegetables from the stove.

Preheat the oven to 200°C/390°F (convection oven 180°C/355°F) and coat an ovenproof dish with olive oil. Now fill the individual shells with the ratatouille vegetables and place one teaspoon of the mascarpone and buffalo mozzarella on top of each of them. Then set the noodles close to each other in the ovenproof dish, put on the middle rack in the oven, and let them gratinate until the cheese melts nicely and the first golden-brown spots appear. This takes about 10–15 minutes.

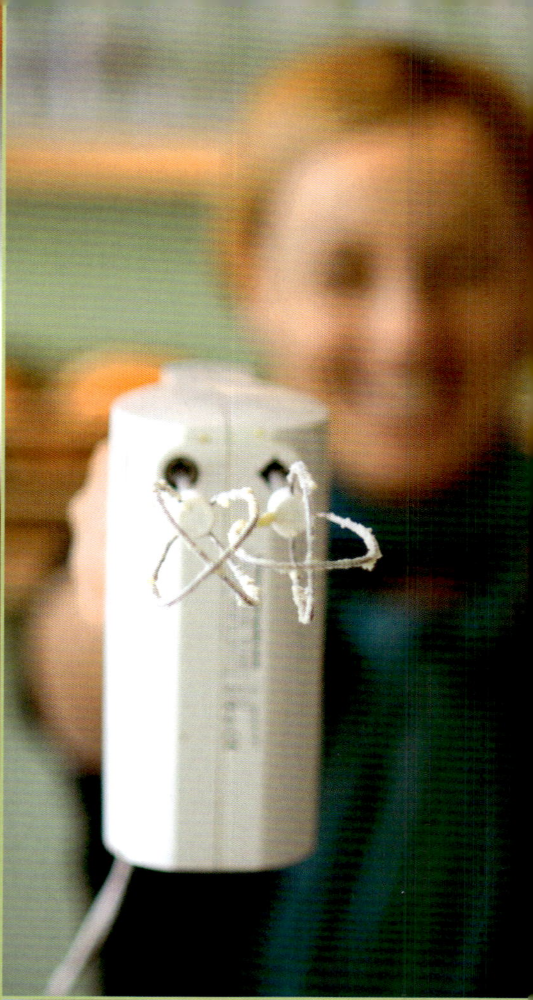

CAFÉ SOLO

While she talks on the phone with a supplier, two espressos hiss from the coffee machine behind her and the cake batter churns through the mixer: multi-tasking is second-nature to Kristin.

Café Solo, Preysingstraße, München/Haidhausen

CAFÉ SOLO

When we moved to Munich in the summer of 2000 (Oliver had just left his job in the USA and I had packed my bags in Regensburg), we had just thought of this city as a stopover. After an almost endless search for an apartment and an odyssey through hotels that went on for months, things finally worked out. We found a place in Haidhausen—also called the French Quarter.

We quickly felt at home here. Haidhausen has many faces because the historic look of the district is enticing for both hipsters and young families. If you let yourself drift through the streets on a sunny summer day, numerous cafés and beer gardens invite you to stop for refreshment. When you go shopping, you stop for a chat with the butcher's wife. If you want to go out in the evening, it's hard to decide because of the long list of cuisines, restaurants, and bars there. Munich may be a big city based on its number of residents, but Haidhausen still gives you a sense of warmth and security. You quickly succumb to its charm.

"Have you already seen what's going on over there where the Chinese fast-food joint used to be? It looks like someone else is moving in there now!" were Oliver's words.

But at the time, we had no idea that the upcoming opening would not only be a café-bar with culinary delicacies, but something like a second living room—including new friends.

During the following weeks, as we walked by we noticed that the formerly unsightly snack-bar was turning into a very inviting all-day bar. We saw a young couple painting and scrubbing enthusiastically, and the friendly colors and new logo were making everyone curious about the opening day. Four years later, Café Solo has become something like an institution in Haidhausen. Kristin now runs the café bar on her own, and her boyfriend Harry helps out when necessary.

If the concept of the "high-powered woman" didn't already exist, it would have to be invented for Kristin.

She manages not only the shopping, accounting, and the daily business with passion. The mother of three very bright children also bakes all of her irresistible cakes and quiches on her own—six days a week! And even though she could compete with any barista behind the coffee machine, Café Solo has little in common with the typical coffee-shop chains.

Kristin knows which guest drinks his Cortado with sugar, who eats his apple cake with whipped cream, and that I don't like pink pepper on my salad.

She has an open ear for the major and minor ailments of her guests and an unbelievable sense of who had a good day and who could use some cheering up. At the same time, her nerves must be made of steel: Not even a play group with babies, dogs that romp through the shop, or an armada of businesspeople can faze her.

"But you don't bake this yourself, do you?" is what new guests always ask after the first bite of Kristin's quiche or cake. They usually just get an impish grin in response from the chef. Instead, she holds her latest creation under my nose for me to try. Things work at least that well in the other direction: My chocolate cake is a regular feature in her cake assortment because we constantly exchange recipes. Yet, the well-known classics such as cheesecake, apple cake, and chocolate cake are what sell like the proverbial hot cakes. But all of her recipes have one thing in common: It must be possible to prepare them in a quick and uncomplicated way. And they have to be an absolute hit when it comes to taste.

KRISTIN'S COLORFUL VEGETABLE QUICHE

Kristin's quiches get the top ratings, especially from the guests who just stop by Café Solo for a quick business lunch. She even has to prepare two additional batches on some days. Served with a crisp salad, they are a light and healthy lunch. Kristin varies the fillings and likes to mix in whatever vegetables are in season at the moment so that the many regulars don't get bored. What are her guests' favorite variations? Green asparagus-carrot-pepper-zucchini and cherry tomatoes-spinach-pear-sheep cheese.

INGREDIENTS

Crust: 125 g/4.5 oz cold butter (plus a bit more for the form) | 125 g/4.5 oz quark (curd cheese, 40% fat) | 1/2 tsp salt | 200 g/7 oz flour (plus a bit more for the form and for kneading) | 3 tbsp breadcrumbs

Filling: about 800 g/1.75 lb cleaned vegetables (such as spinach, asparagus, carrots, zucchini, and onions) | 2 tbsp olive oil | 2 tbsp freshly chopped herbs | salt | freshly ground pepper
Topping: 200 g/7 oz sour cream or crème fraîche | 2 tbsp flour | 50 g/1.75 oz grated cheese (such as Gouda) | 6 large eggs | salt | freshly ground pepper

PREPARATION

For the crust, cut the butter into cubes and put into a bowl with the curd cheese, salt, and flour. Quickly work into a dough by hand or with the food processor, but don't knead any longer than necessary. Wrap in foil and cool for 30 minutes.

For the filling, dice the vegetables and sauté in oil over medium heat until half cooked. Add the herbs and season with salt and pepper. Remove from the stove and leave to cool. For the topping, mix cream or crème fraîche and add the flour, cheese, and eggs. Season with salt and pepper.

Preheat the oven to 190°C/375°F (convection oven 170°C/340°F). Butter a spring form (26 cm/10 inch Ø) and dust with flour. Roll out the dough and evenly line the form with it (4 cm/1 .5 inch edge). Prick the bottom in a number of places with a fork and spread the breadcrumbs on it. Now add the vegetables to the egg mixture and then pour into the form. Bake in the oven on the second-lowest rack for 35–40 minutes until the edge has a golden-brown color and the filling shows brown spots, which means that the quiche is ready. If it turns dark too quickly, cover it with some parchment paper. It tastes good warm or cold with a fresh salad.

CHEESECAKE À LA CAFÉ SOLO

It isn't that easy to find a good cheesecake in Munich. They are frequently rather dry or simply too sweet. That's why I was even more surprised when Kristin presented me with the new item in the cake assortment.

I thought the fact that she used full-fat curd cheese (quark) instead of low-fat was especially great–and that's also precisely how the cake tastes: wonderfully creamy, slightly tart, and just very easy to fall in love with!

I proclaimed the following week as my personal cheesecake week. I visited Kristin in the café every day from Monday to Friday in order to secure my individual daily ration of the cake. Thank God, she showed some compassion and gave me her recipe!

INGREDIENTS

Dough: 125 g/4.5 oz soft butter (plus a bit more for the form) | 1 small egg (room temperature) | 60g/2 oz sugar | 200 g/7 oz flour (plus 2 tbsp for kneading)

Filling: 750 g/1.65 lb curd cheese (40% fat, or simple curd cheese as a substitute) | about 5 tbsp vanilla pudding powder (not instant) | 120 g/4.25 oz sugar | juice of 1 lemon | 5 large eggs | 125 g/ 4.5 oz melted butter | seeds of 1/2 vanilla pod (optional)

PREPARATION

Preheat oven to 175°C/345°F (convection oven 160°C/320°F). Grease a spring form (26 cm/ 10 inch Ø) with butter.

Put the ingredients for the dough in a bowl and first mix with the kneading hooks of the hand-mixer. Then knead by hand into a ball on the floured countertop. The dough should be so soft that you don't have to roll it out, but just press it directly into the form with your fingers, which is quite easy. As you do this, shape an even edge of 3–4 cm/about 1.25–1.5 inches high and prick the bottom a few times with a fork.

Now mix the ingredients for the filling well with the whisk of the hand-mixer in a large bowl and pour onto the crust.

Bake the cake in the oven on the second-lowest rack for about 45 minutes. The edge of the short pastry should be golden brown, and the filling should already feel relatively firm under the pressure of a finger. Remove from the oven and let cool completely in the form.

quick & easy

INDIAN BREAD SALAD

Once in a while you experience one of these enlightening moments while cooking. You use the ingredients in a combination that is new to you and ask yourself at the same time why this fantastic idea didn't occur to you before. That's what happened to me with this salad. The original version was a recipe by Tanja Dusy, who is a successful cookbook author and expert on Indian cuisine. The crisp croutons that already exude an indescribable Far-Eastern aroma in my kitchen when roasted in cumin and garam masala are the main attraction here. This is my favorite salad, and I just love to eat my share of it.

SERVES 4
PREPARATION TIME: 30 MINUTES

300 g/10.5 oz cherry tomatoes
1 cucumber
1 red onion
1 large red chili pepper
1 can of garbanzo beans (240 g/8.5 oz drained)
6 tbsp canola oil (or any other vegetable oil)
2 tbsp white wine vinegar
1/2 tsp sugar
Salt
Freshly ground black pepper
1/4 bunch of cilantro
1/4 bunch of mint
200 g/7 oz flat unleavened bread
5 tbsp ghee (Indian clarified butter or substitute with normal clarified butter)
1 tbsp cumin seeds
1 tbsp garam masala (Indian spice mixture)
4 tbsp Greek yogurt (optional)

Wash and cut the cherry tomatoes into quarters. Wash the cucumber and cut crosswise into two halves, then divide each of the halves again lengthwise. Scratch the seeds out with a teaspoon. Cut each cucumber quarter lengthwise into four equal strips and then into finger-thick pieces. Peel the onion and dice finely. Wash the chili pepper, remove the stem, and chop finely. Pour the garbanzo beans into a sieve, rinse with cold water, and let drain. Then mix all of the ingredients in a bowl.

For the dressing, mix the canola oil, white wine vinegar, sugar, salt, and pepper. Rinse off the herbs, shake dry, chop until fine, and blend in. Mix the dressing into the salad, cover, and marinate for about
20 minutes (but if you are hungry, 5 minutes are long enough).

In the meantime, cut the flat, unleavened bread into thumb-thick cubes. Heat the ghee in a pan. Grind the cumin finely in a mortar and put into the pan together with the garam masala. Now add the croutons and roast evenly while stirring over medium heat until they are golden-brown and crisp.

Divide the salad into four little bowls and arrange with the croutons. If you like, you can add a dollop of the Greek yogurt to each bowl (it may not be typically Indian, but goes extremely well with it).

THE BEST CHEESE SPAETZLE

I ever ate was at a ski lodge many years ago in the Salzburger Land. The chunky little buttons steamed with promise from a heavy small iron pan, buried beneath a mountain of golden-brown fried onions. Every time I speared them with my fork, I pulled up long threads of cheese. It really was pure joy.

Of course, any meal that you eat when you're ravenous and—at least in my case—have set in front of you at a ski lodge when you have cold feet is the best one that you can imagine at that moment. But this reminiscent thought has stayed with me for a long time. Could it be that hard to make these spaetzle at home?

SERVES 4
PREPARATION TIME: 45 MINUTES

Spaetzle

500 g/1.1 lb flour
10 medium eggs
2 medium egg whites
Salt
50 g/1.75 oz butter
150–200 g/5.25–7 oz freshly grated cheese (Bergkäse, Emmentaler, or Appenzeller)

Garnish

3 large onions
1 tbsp flour
1/2 tsp salt
100 g/3.5 oz butter
1 small bunch of chives

Plus

Spaetzle maker

For the spaetzle, vigorously beat the flour, eggs, egg yolks, salt and 3 tbsp of water with a wooden spoon in a large bowl (or use a food processor and kneading hooks) for at least 5 minutes until bubbles form and there are no more little lumps in the dough. If necessary, add water by the tablespoon until the dough falls heavily from the spoon. The dough should also taste slightly salty, but this goes away after boiling. Let stand for 15 minutes.

In the meantime, peel the onions for the garnish. Cut them into fine rings and dust with flour and salt. Let the butter foam in a large pan and slowly fry the rings over low to medium heat until they are golden-brown, but don't let them get too dark (because that makes them taste bitter). Drain on paper towels. Wash the chives, shake dry, and dice.

Boil water in a large pot and add plenty of salt. Then reduce the heat until the water is just slightly simmering. Grate the dough bit by bit into the water with a spaetzle maker and let the spaetzle cook briefly until they rise to the surface. Then take them out with a slotted spoon, put them into a colander, and rinse quickly with cold water (prevents them from sticking together).

When you have used all the dough, pour the cooking water over the spaetzle (warms them up again). Place the pot back on the stove and let the butter melt over medium heat. Then add the drained spaetzle. Stir in the cheese (it tastes best when you use a mixture of various types) until it melts and gets stringy. Serve the cheese spaetzle with the roasted onions and chives. The perfect side dish: a large bowl of green salad.

To bake them in the oven, layer the finished spaetzle with the cheese in a buttered ovenproof dish and bake in a 200°C/390°F oven (convection oven 180°C/355°F) for about 10–15 minutes.

GRATIN OF BELGIAN ENDIVE

Sometimes all you need is a good recipe and a new preparation method to overcome all of your aversions to a certain ingredient. It's not that I didn't try—for years, Belgian endives had wandered into my shopping basket time and again. The idea that these little heads of lettuce can be cleaned in the shortest time was very tempting. But I still could never really be enthusiastic about Belgian endives in a salad because I felt their taste was simply too bitter.

But Belgian endive au gratin? It's as if it took off its homely duds and put on a really fancy evening gown! The Pancetta gives it a spicy touch and the coarsely crumbled white bread and Parmesan provide a crisp topping. This will easily turn anyone into a fan of Belgian endive.

SERVES 4
PREPARATION TIME: 15 MINUTES
PLUS 15–25 MINUTES FOR GRATINATING

Olive oil for brushing and sprinkling
8 small Belgian endives
3–4 tbsp sugar
Coarse sea salt
Freshly ground black pepper
100 g/3.5 oz butter
100 g/3.5 oz Pancetta (but another type of bacon works just as well)
100 g/3.5 oz white bread (from the previous day)
50 g/1.75 oz freshly grated Parmesan
2–3 tbsp pine nuts (optional)
3 thyme sprigs

Preheat the oven to 180°C/355°F (convection oven 160°C/320°F) and brush a large ovenproof dish or a baking sheet with olive oil.

Remove the outer and wilted leaves of the endives, wash the heads if necessary, and then halve lengthwise. Place in the ovenproof dish or on the baking sheet with the cut sides up. Sprinkle with the sugar and 1 pinch each of salt and pepper. Place butter in little flakes on top of each piece. Cut the bacon into thin strips and also sprinkle it over the Belgian endive. Bake everything in the oven on the middle rack for 10–15 minutes until the bacon looks a bit crispy.

In the meantime, grind the white bread into coarse crumbs in the food processor (or cut into very small pieces with a knife) and mix with the Parmesan and the pine nuts. Rinse off the thyme, shake dry, and strip the small leaves from the sprigs.

Remove Belgian endives from the oven and increase the temperature to 200°C/390°F (convection oven 180°C/355°F). Generously spread the Parmesan crumbs over the Belgian endive halves, sprinkle with the small thyme leaves, and add a few splashes of olive oil. Brown for another 5–10 minutes in the oven. (I usually also turn on the grill so that the gratin turns a nice color. But if you do this, be sure to keep a constant eye on it so that it doesn't get too dark.) Enjoy it on its own or with boiled potatoes.

ANTI-HANGOVER SALAD

Even though the party was out of this world, you quickly realize that you could have done without one or two of those drinks when you wake up with an aching head the next morning. Hello, hangover! My appetite usually goes into hiding as well. The right food can actually help to revive you more quickly. But who really wants to eat raw eggs and rolled pickled herring?

On the other hand, this herring salad can be prepared in no time—because it really isn't fun to stand around in the kitchen for a long time with a hangover—and it quickly supplies your body with the minerals and proteins that it desperately needs in this situation. The original recipe comes from Petra Holzapfel, a friend of mine who is a food-blogger in the Bavarian Forest. Her blog, "Chili and Ciabatta" (www.peho.typepad.com) is a website that I visit on a regular basis to whet my appetite because her recipes are both creative and down-to-earth. Quite a few of them even have strong potential to become favorites—like this anti-hangover salad (of course, it also tastes good without the hangover).

SERVES 4
PREPARATION TIME: 20 MINUTES
PLUS 1 HOUR FOR MARINATING

3–4 dill stalks
200 g/7 oz sour cream or crème fraîche
100 g/3.5 oz whipping cream
1 tbsp lemon juice
1/2 tsp sugar
Salt
Freshly ground black pepper
Freshly grated nutmeg
1 large red onion
100 g/3.5 oz cornichons (pickled gherkins)
2 tart apples (such as Granny Smiths)
400 g/14 oz Bismarck herring fillets

For the salad cream, rinse off the dill, shake dry, and finely mince the tips. Combine in a large bowl with the sour cream or crème fraîche and the whipping cream. Season to taste with the lemon juice, sugar, plenty of salt, pepper, and nutmeg.

Peel the onion and dice it finely. Slice the pickles. Quarter, core, and peel the apples and cut them into fine slices. Divide the Bismarck herring fillets lengthwise and cut into finger-thick strips.

Mix the onion, pickles, apple, and Bismarck herring fillets into the salad cream. Cover and let marinate for about 1 hour in the refrigerator. Also goes well with boiled potatoes.

EMERGENCY PASTA

The window sill in our kitchen is tremendously functional for its small size. To the right and left of it, almost a dozen different wooden and plastic cutting boards in all sizes and colors lean against the wall. The rest of the space is shared by a water boiler, a blender, various pots with herbs—that sometimes look fresh and sometimes not so fresh—and two fruit baskets that are usually filled to the top. Two? My weakness for fresh lemons and limes, which are simply indispensible in my kitchen, is to blame. The supply is sometimes so large that we could have an impromptu Caipirinha party. That's because many dishes can be refined with citrus. Untreated organic fruit is optimal because you don't have to worry about using its zest.

When I don't need the limes to season individual dishes or for homemade lemonade (see page 194), then there's a good chance that they will serve as an ingredient in my Emergency Pasta. Or, to put it differently: I don't have the time or inspiration to cook but still want to have a large plate of steaming pasta. It's so simple and so good...

SERVES 2 (AND NOT 4 BECAUSE YOU ONLY MAKE THE EMERGENCY PASTA FOR YOURSELF, NOT FOR GUESTS)
PREPARATION TIME: 15 MINUTES

250 g/9 oz spaghetti
Salt
1 organic lime

To taste
Freshly ground, dried chili peppers
Freshly ground black pepper
Good quality olive oil
Freshly grated Parmesan

For the spaghetti, bring plenty of water to a boil in a large pot. Add a generous amount of salt to the water and boil the pasta according to the package instructions until cooked but firm to the bite (al dente). Finally, drain in a colander and reserve some of the cooking water. Put the pasta back into the pot.

Wash the lime with hot water and finely grate the zest directly over the pasta. Cut the lime in half, squeeze it, and also sprinkle the juice over the pasta. Season to taste with chili and pepper. Slash with a bit of the reserved pasta water and plenty of olive oil. Then shake the pot well or mix the pasta with a cooking spoon. They should be coated very evenly with the sauce and spices so that they have a silky shine to them.

Instead of salt, "season" the pasta with a generous amounts of freshly grated Parmesan. Enjoy immediately!

INDIAN-STYLE SQUASH SOUP

If the weather outside is cold and stormy, I can't help but dream about a large bowl of hot soup. Whether as comfort food or to warm the belly—it can help end any rainy day on an upbeat note. One of the top choices on my list is this velvety squash soup with a taste that will subtly remind you of an Indian curry. Although my very favorite one of them all is the butternut squash with its fine, nutty aroma; a Kabucha squash or muscat pumpkin are just as suitable for this quick recipe.

SERVES 4
PREPARATION TIME: 30 MINUTES

1 squash (such as butternut squash, about 600 g/1.3 lb)
1 onion
1 garlic clove
1 piece of fresh ginger (about 2 cm/ 0.75 inch)
2 tbsp ghee (Indian clarified butter or substitute with normal clarified butter)
2–3 tsp curry paste (such as Indian garam masala paste)
400 ml/13.5 fl oz coconut milk
600 ml/20 fl oz vegetable stock
Sea salt
2 tbsp brown mustard seeds

Cut the squash into slices, remove the seeds, and then peel it—this is the easiest way to do it. If peeling is too much work for you, then just pick a type of squash that doesn't need to be peeled (such as the Kabucha). Cut the squash into medium-sized cubes.

Peel the onion and garlic clove and mince finely. Peel the ginger and chop (or grate) finely. Melt the ghee over a medium heat in a large pot. Cook the onion and garlic until glassy, then add the squash pieces. Add the ginger and curry paste, browning briefly until its aroma tickles your nose.

Pour in the coconut milk and vegetable stock. Simmer for about 15 minutes until the squash pieces can be easily mashed with a fork. Puree the soup with an immersion blender until it's smooth and season with salt.

Brown the mustard seeds in a pan without fat until they start to crackle, then add to the finished squash soup. The best way to serve it is with flat unleavened bread and sour cream.

ASIAN SESAME-CHICKEN SALAD

Like many of the old buildings in Haidhausen, our house has a small, peaceful courtyard that is degraded to a place for parking bicycles during most of the year. But it is cleared out and spruced up for one weekend in the summer—that's when we have a house party! All of the residents get together on this weekend to have a feast and everyone contributes one or two homemade delicacies from their own kitchens: Martina and Ruth are famous for their cakes, Gitti's cold apple soup with chili and mint had everyone raving last time, and their lordships manage the barbecue. In between, we share the latest gossip from the neighborhood and obviously laugh a lot. This is a cherished tradition that I wouldn't want to miss. Even when our neighbors like to try and test new recipes, this salad with an Asian touch is so popular that I have to bring it with me time and again.

SERVES 4
PREPARATION TIME: 40 MINUTES

500 g/1.1 lb chicken breast fillets
Salt
1 cucumber
1/2 large red chili pepper
3 tbsp peanut oil
1–2 tsp Szechuan pepper
5 tbsp sesame seeds
1 garlic clove
4 tbsp Kejap Manis (Indonesian sweet soy sauce)
4 tbsp sesame oil (plus a bit extra for sprinkling)
100 g/3.5 oz dried Japanese noodles (such as Somen or Soba)

Wash the chicken breast fillets and place in a pot with lightly salted water. Bring to a boil, reduce the heat, and the cook the fillets in the slightly simmering water for 10–15 minutes until done (to test, cut to see whether they are completely cooked). Take the fillets out of the water, wrap in foil, and let cool for a while.

Wash the cucumber, cut in half lengthwise, and remove the seeds with a teaspoon. Cut the cucumber diagonally into thin slices. Wash the chili, remove the stem, and cut into fine rings. Heat the peanut oil with the chili and Szechuan pepper in a pan until the pepper unfolds its aroma. Add the cucumber and salt. Simmer for about 5 minutes over medium heat, remove from the pan, and let cool.

Briefly toast sesame seeds in a dry pan until shiny. Peel the garlic and crush in a mortar with 4 tbsp of the sesame seeds. Add the rest of the sesame seeds, Kejap Manis, sesame oil, and about 5 tbsp of water and stir. Shred the cooked chicken meat, mix into the sauce, and marinate briefly.

Cook the noodles according to the package instructions, drain in a colander, and rinse off with cold water. Mix the noodles with the cucumber, divide into small bowls, and top with the marinated chicken meat. Sprinkle with a bit of the sesame oil to taste.

TOMATO SUGO WITH FENNEL

You would think that something as simple as a tomato sauce for pasta would be easy to whip up. But there are a few basic questions that arise for some cooks: Should you use butter or is olive oil better? Fresh tomatoes or canned? Some sugar, many herbs, aromatic garlic, colorful vegetables or just very simple? In my opinion, there is no single true variation. Depending on what's in my cupboards and what I feel like eating, I usually decide spontaneously what will go into the pan. Tomatoes, however, are the only ingredient for which there is no way out here. A fruity sauce cannot be made from fres tomatoes if they are watery—even with the best of intentions. No, in this case, you are still better off with top-class canned tomatoes (the best pomodori pelati come from San Marzano).

SERVES 4
PREPARATION TIME: 30 MINUTES

1 large onion
2 garlic cloves
1 large red chili pepper
300 g/10.5 oz fennel (definitely with their rich fronds)
800 g/1.75 lb canned tomatoes (with the juice)
3 tbsp olive oil
150 ml/5 fl oz vodka
100 g/3.5 oz whipping cream
1 tbsp sugar
Sea salt
Freshly ground black pepper
500 g/1.1 lb pasta (such as penne or rigatoni)
150 g/5.25 oz cherry tomatoes

Peel and finely dice the onion and the garlic. Wash the chili pepper, remove the stem, and mince finely. (If you like, you can remove the especially hot seeds and fibers in advance. Be sure to wash your fingers thoroughly afterward!) Wash and clean the fennel, cut off the green fronds and save for later use. Cut the fennel into quarters lengthwise and then cut these into thin slices. Pour the canned tomatoes into a colander and save the juice. Chop the tomatoes coarsely. If necessary, remove the base of the stems as you do this.

Heat the olive oil in a large pan. Brown the onion and garlic in it over medium heat. Add the chili and fennel slices. Sauté for about 5 minutes but make sure that the vegetables in the pan don't change color. Pour in the vodka and mix in the canned tomatoes with their juice, as well as the whipping cream. Season with sugar, salt, and pepper. Let the sugo simmer lightly for about 20 minutes until it reduces in volume.

In the meantime, put on a large pot with plenty of water for the pasta and let it boil. Add a generous amount of salt to the water and cook the pasta according to the package instructions until firm to the bite. Wash the cherry tomatoes, cut into quarters, and let simmer for the last 1–2 minutes in the sugo.

Finely chop the fennel fronds that you set aside (it should be about 4 tbsp), and stir half of them into the sauce. Drain the pasta and mix with the sauce. Sprinkle the rest of the fennel fronds on top before serving.

HANDE'S SESAME POTATOES WITH TZATZIKI

My friend Hande is a phenomenon when it comes to the topic of cooking and eating. Widely traveled, well-read, and endowed with a healthy amount of curiosity, there is almost nothing that she doesn't know or hasn't tried. She likes to bring us newly discovered spices from her trips, and sometimes also supplies the appropriate recipes with them—as in this case. Unfortunately, the little glass jar with the spice mixture from Granada has now been used up. So this is a good reason for me to mix my own trimmed-down version.

The sesame potatoes are not only a pleasure as a side dish for roasted meat. I also like to serve them as a quickly prepared everyday meal together with a large bowl of tzatziki.

SERVES 4
PREPARATION TIME: 30 MINUTES
PLUS 30–40 MINUTES FOR BAKING

Tzatziki

1 large cucumber | salt
2–3 garlic cloves
500 g/1.1 lb Greek yogurt
2 tbsp olive oil
Freshly ground black pepper

Sesame Potatoes

1 tsp cumin seeds
1 tsp coriander seeds
1/2 tsp turmeric powder
1/4 tsp cayenne pepper
Freshly grated nutmeg
1 kg/2.2 lb small waxy potatoes (La Ratte are wonderful)
Olive oil for brushing and coating
5 tbsp sesame seeds
Coarse sea salt
Medium-hot, smoked paprika powder (Pimentón de la Vera)

For the tzatziki, wash the cucumber, cut in half lengthwise, remove the seeds with a teaspoon, and grate. Put the grated cucumber into a colander, salt well, and let steep for at least 5 minutes. Peel the garlic, finely mince, and put into a bowl together with the yogurt. Squeeze liquid out of the grated cucumber and mix into the yogurt. Season the tzatziki to taste with the olive oil, salt (if still necessary), and pepper. Let marinate in the refrigerator until the potatoes are done.

For the sesame potatoes, preheat the oven to 200°C/390°F. Finely grind cumin, coriander, turmeric, and cayenne pepper with a generous pinch of nutmeg in the mortar. Wash the potatoes and cut in half lengthwise. They will be done more quickly and evenly if you cut into their skins. This is very easy to do: Place each potato half with the cut surface facing downward between two wooden chopsticks and cut into them. The chopsticks will prevent you from inadvertently cutting all the way through them.

Grease a baking sheet with olive oil and sprinkle with sesame seeds. Place the potatoes on the sheet with the cut sides down. Brush them with olive oil and then sprinkle with sea salt, paprika powder, and the freshly prepared spice mixture. Put the sheet on the middle rack in the oven (180°C/355°F convection oven) and bake the potatoes until they are golden-brown and crisp, which takes about 30–40 minutes (depending on the size of the potatoes). Turn once while they bake.

GORGONZOLA RISOTTO

Who actually started the rumor that risotto is difficult to prepare? I can understand these reservations for some dishes, but certainly not for risotto. If the ingredients are right and you can give the pot of rice your full attention for just about 30 minutes and stir regularly, then you can put a wonderful meal on the table in little more than half an hour. And once you have learned the basic technique, there isn't anything to stop you from experimenting with the various ingredients. That's exactly how I created this recipe, which is quite a treat for risotto fans. The sweetness of the apple and the onions coax the finest aromas out of the Gorgonzola and show it from its very best side.

SERVES 4
PREPARATION TIME: 30 MINUTES

- 4 tbsp butter
- 250 g/9 oz risotto rice (such as Vialone Nano)
- About 1 l/1 US quart of hot vegetable stock
- 2 small onions
- 2 sweet-tart apples
- Freshly grated nutmeg
- Salt
- 100 g/3.5 oz Gorgonzola dolce
- 30 g/1 oz freshly grated Parmesan (plus a bit more for serving)
- 2 tbsp Calvados (optional)

Let 2 tbsp of butter foam in a large pan. Add the rice and sauté it until glossy while stirring. Pour in some vegetable stock. Continue to stir and keep adding stock until the rice is covered by it. Simmer for about 20 minutes over small to medium heat until soft (the risotto rice tells the cook how much liquid it needs and not the other way around). Keep tasting the rice just before it's almost done.

In the meantime, peel the onions and finely dice them. Let the rest of the butter foam in a pan. Add the onions and slowly brown over medium heat. Cut the apples into quarters, core, and peel. Then cut into thin slices and small pieces. Add the apples to the onions in the pan and season with nutmeg and a bit of salt. Sauté mixture for about 5 minutes and then keep it warm on the stove over the lowest heat.

As soon as the rice has a very slight bite to it, add the Gorgonzola and Parmesan. Let the cheese melt as you mix it in. Stir in half of the sautéed onion—apple mixture and season to taste with Calvados (optional) and salt. The risotto should have a velvety, slightly flowing consistency. If not, pour in a bit more stock. Arrange on the plate and sprinkle with the rest of the sautéed onion-apple mixture and some Parmesan.

FRESH MEA
SANDWICHE
CE CREAM
WINE

ROADTRIP USA

»If you don't like the food in the States,
you probably have the wrong friends.«

David Kunstle

ROADTRIP USA

When I fell head over heels in love with Oliver, Cupid put a spoke in the wheels in two different ways: Not only had I lost my heart to someone for whom cooking was absolutely new territory; the timing was even worse. Just the day before, Oliver had signed a contract with his old company in the USA—we had less than three weeks together before he had to fly back to America. Resigning to our fate, we decided to make the best of the situation and were working on plans for my next semester break when my parents surprised me with a ticket. I was to spend Christmas and New Year in Atlanta!

This first trip was followed by many more and we spent a wonderfully carefree time together.

While I made sure that Oliver's refrigerator was filled with more than just Corona, milk, and ice cubes and his kitchen was really used for cooking every once in a while, he constantly came up with new outings to help me appreciate this diverse country. Whenever his job allowed it, we packed only what was absolutely necessary, said a quick prayer so that his beloved old convertible wouldn't leave us in the lurch, and set out on our way. Our very first route on the East Coast to Savannah and Charleston enchanted me: Overhanging trees covered with thick Spanish moss and historic streets lined with colonial-style houses radiated the charm of the South. We felt transported back to a time long gone, and the clocks there actually seemed to tick a little more slowly.

I quickly learned that the distances in the USA are actually very different from those in Germany. It wasn't unusual for us to spend half the day on the highway before we reached the next destination. I've been fascinated about this type of traveling ever since—always following your nose and discovering the land and people without much planning. We spent nights in motels worthy of David Lynch, under the open sky, or in quirky bed-and-breakfasts, assembled giant sandwiches on the hood of our car, always searched for the best burger, and couldn't drive by any of the farmers' markets without stopping. At the same time, every region was so different. We were curious about the great diversity of multicultural influences and culinary traditions that were waiting to be discovered.

My most beautiful memories always include the days and weeks that we spent with friends and their families, during which almost everything is focused on cooking and eating—there's hardly a better way to get to know the regional cuisine with its special features. When visiting Sherry and Bob in California, I can always envious of the variety of fruits and vegetables you could grow in your garden there:

Sun-warmed peaches ripen next to Meyer lemons (which are unfamiliar in Germany) or figs. If you wander through the luxuriantly blossoming garden, you can quickly nibble on an entire handful of wild strawberries that are as sweet as sugar.

Several days, many highway miles and breathtaking canyons later, we have the alternative program in Colorado. Stephanie and David had lived in our neighborhood in Munich for quite a while before they returned to their homeland. Every time we visit, we are once again overwhelmed by the hospitality of their families. Whenever an opportunity arises, they get together to cook, barbecue, and party. Now that they have let us in on the family secrets of their fantastic tamales, chili rellenos, and sopapillas, we do certainly like to return the favor and acquaint them with our traditional Bavarian dishes.

Not just the way to a man's heart is through the stomach, but also the path to friendship!

END
CALIFORNIA
136

TAMALES
À LA GRANDMOTHER SALAZAR

Whenever Stephanie talks about her grandmother, her dark eyes sparkle and you quickly notice how passionately everything revolves around cooking and eating in her family:

"Whatever Grandmother Salazar prepares, it's simply indescribably delicious! She already baked her first cookies for her father as a child barely being able to reach the stove and standing on a chair. Unfortunately, her parents passed away very early and she was forced to provide for her seven siblings and all of the farm workers when they came home from the fields. She served them steaming bean stew and giant piles of homemade tortillas."

Tamales originated in Mexico but have a long tradition on the American continent. Depending on the region, they have a variety of fillings that are wrapped in corn husks or banana leaves and steamed. Their preparation is time-consuming and somewhat arduous, but you can easily freeze them for future occasions.. People like to use tamales as a reason for gathering the entire family and friends around the kitchen table to produce true mountains of them for holidays or special occasions.

This recipe makes about 70 tamales, but the quantities can easily be cut in half (the amount of garlic and onions doesn't change, however). If you prefer, you can also just use either pork or beef in them.

INGREDIENTS

2 large onions | 4 garlic cloves | plenty of chili powder | 1.5 kg/3.3 lb of pork and beef each (suitable for roasting in the oven or braising) | salt | freshly ground pepper | corn husks (2–3 packages, available at Mexican stores or online) | ground cumin (optional) | about 1 kg/2.2 lb cornmeal (Masa Harina) | 200 g/7 oz lard

PREPARATION: DAY 1

Put two large pots with water on the stove and add 1 peeled onion, 2 peeled garlic cloves, and 1 tsp of chili powder to each of them. Bring the water in both pots to a boil. Then add one type of meat to each pot and gently simmer covered over low heat for at least 4 hours until it almost falls apart. Take the meat out of the broth and let it cool. Then shred it using your fingers or two forks. Place in refrigerator covered until needed.

Purée one of the broths with the cooked onions and garlic cloves. Use the other broth how ever you want to. Then season with salt, pepper, and some more chili powder. Store the broth in the refrigerator.

Soak the corn husks overnight in plenty of water.

PREPARATION: DAY 2

Rinse the corn husks under running water and dry off, which is best done by placing them on kitchen towels. Strongly season the shredded meat with chili powder, salt, and cumin (optional) and mix well. If you moisten the meat a little with the broth that you prepared, the spices mix in more easily.

Knead the cornmeal together with the lard, about 4 tsp salt, and plenty of chili powder (should be noticeable in the color of the dough!) with your hands to make the dough. Add tablespoons of the broth so that the dough is smooth and can be easily spread onto the corn husks later.

Now spread a thin layer of the corn dough (Masa) on a corn husk, leaving several centimeters/about an inch free as a border along the sides. Spread about 2 tbsp of the meat on it and wrap the Masa around it, just like a cigar. Now fold the corn husks over it (if the borders are too wide, you can easily tear the strips off) and tuck in the ends.

Stephanie's grandmother uses thin strips of the corn husks, decoratively tying the tamales with bows into pretty little packages.

Now fill a wok with 5 cm/2 inches of water and bring to a boil. Place the tamales in a bamboo steaming basket (they are inexpensive and available at Asian stores) and cover. Place the basket in

the wok and steam the tamales for 15–20 minutes until they are done and can easily be removed from the corn husk. (For frozen tamales, just let them steam 5 minutes longer without defrosting in advance.)

SHERRY'S GALETTE

I always thought that galettes were French buckwheat pancakes until our American friends served them to us in a completely different look. Sherry's variation can be prepared in countless versions and requires almost no effort. Once you have the hang of it, you will be rewarded with the lightest, flakiest short pastry that you can imagine. This is a genuine all-round recipe that I sometimes like to fill with plums and sometimes with pears or nectarines, depending on the season. Even fruit that has seen better days can be included.

INGREDIENTS

Dough (for 2 galettes, each about 22 cm/8.75 inch Ø): 175 g/6 oz flour | 1 tbsp white sugar | 1/4 tsp salt | 100 g/3.5 oz cold butter (in small pieces) | 1 tbsp sour cream

Filling (for 1 galette): 300–400 g/10.5–14 oz fruit (such as pears, nectarines, plums, apples, blueberries, or apricots) , cleaned and cut into small pieces | 1 tbsp chopped nuts (optional) | 1–2 tbsp raw cane sugar | 1 tbsp cold butter (in small pieces)

Plus (for 1 galette): 100 g/ 3.5 oz crème fraîche | 2 tbsp raw cane sugar | confectioner's sugar to taste

PREPARATION

For the dough, put the flour, sugar, salt, and butter into a food processor equipped with the cutting blade. Blend at short intervals (pulse function) until the mixture looks like coarse bread crumbs. Mix the whipping cream and 50 ml/1.75 fl oz of ice-cold water. Add little by little, always just briefly combining everything. To prepare the dough by hand: Mix the flour, sugar, and salt in a bowl. Work in the butter as quickly as possible: use an American pastry cutter or smash the pieces of butter into the flour with your fingers until they are pea-sized crumbs. Mix the sour cream and water, then add one tablespoon at a time and repeatedly mix all of the ingredients with a fork.

The dough should now be moist and firm enough to be shaped into a ball (if not, then add either the flour or the ice-cold water by the tablespoon)–but be sure not to knead it too much. Any small pieces of butter will make sure that the dough will be nice and flaky later. Divide the dough in half, shape roughly into two finger-thick round disks. Wrap in foil and let it become firm for at least 1 hour in the refrigerator. The dough will also keep there for several days.

Preheat the oven to 180°C/355°F (convection oven 160°C/320°F). Lightly dust one of the chilled dough rounds with flour (save the other one to bake later) and roll out to a thickness of about 3 mm/0.1 inch. Drape around a rolling pin, put on

a baking sheet covered with baking paper, and fill: Cover with the fruit, but leave a border of about 5 cm/2 inches. If you like, you can now top with the nuts. Sprinkle with 1 tbsp raw cane sugar and distribute the pieces of butter. Fold the dough border toward the filling–it's fine if it looks a bit rustic. Then brush with water and sprinkle a bit of raw cane sugar on top. Put on the middle rack in the hot oven.

Before serving, mix the crème fraîche and raw cane sugar. Leave for 10 minutes until the sugar crystals have dissolved, then stir thoroughly again. This gives the crème a subtle caramel flavor that harmonizes well with the fruit.

After 30–40 minutes, the border of the galette will have a golden-brown color and the fruit will be soft. Take out of the oven, cut into portions, and serve with a spoon of crème fraîche while still warm. If you like, you can dust the galette with a little confectioner's sugar–and it's ready!

elegant & extravagant

GRAVED CHAR WITH HONEY-MUSTARD DRESSING

Marinated fish is great to prepare in advance and guaranteed to make an impression—you don't have to let your guests know how easy it actually is to make. Just removing the bones takes some patience. Fresh salmon is normally used for this recipe, but my personal favorites are char and trout because they have a somewhat subtler taste.

SERVES 4 AS AN APPETIZER
PREPARATION TIME: 30 MINUTES
PLUS 24 HOURS MARINATING TIME

Graved Char

2 char fillets with skin (150 g/5.25oz each)
2 organic limes
1 tsp black peppercorns
2 tbsp coarse sea salt
1 tbsp sugar
1 piece of fresh ginger (about 3 cm/ 1.25 inch)
The fronds of 1–2 fennel bulbs

Dressing

4 tbsp olive oil
2 tbsp orange juice
1 tbsp white wine vinegar
1 tbsp mild honey
1/2 tsp Dijon mustard
Sea salt (if necessary)

Wash the fish fillets and dab them dry. Use your fingers to carefully feel for any bones and remove them with a pair of tweezers. Place fillets with the skin side down on the countertop.

Wash the limes with hot water, finely grate the zest, and sprinkle over the fillets. Coarsely grind the peppercorns in the mortar, mix with the coarse sea salt and sugar, and sprinkle evenly over the fillets. Peel the ginger and cut into thin slices. Wash the fennel fronds, shake dry, and chop finely. Sprinkle both over a fillet. Place the other fillet with the seasoned side facing up.

Fillets prepared in this way are usually put into a dish that is big enough to hold all the fish, covered with foil, and then have a weight placed on them. My variation saves space: Fold the fillets and wrap tightly in plastic foil, then wrap in newspaper. Marinate fillets in the refrigerator for 24 hours. After about 12 hours, turn once so that the marinade is evenly distributed. Then unpack the fillets and remove the ginger.

Either cut the fillets with all of the herbs and spices into slices that are as thin as possible or—if the char is too spicy otherwise—rinse the fish under cold running water, dab dry (if you like, you can sprinkle the fillets again with freshly chopped fennel fronds) and then cut into thin slices. Serve with the dressing.

Dressing: Briefly mix all of the ingredients in a tall container with the hand-held blender and season to taste. Graved char is quite salty, which is why I often don't add any salt to it.

WILD MUSHROOM SOUP WITH WALNUT RAVIOLI

If you have ever prepared filled pasta, you know that these little handmade delicacies are a true labor of love. This is why they are only on my menu when I have the time and leisure, but then...

SERVES 4 AS A LIGHT ENTRÉE
PREPARATION TIME: 1 1/2 HOURS

Dough
150 g/5.25 oz flour
1/4 tsp salt
1 medium egg
2–3 medium egg yolks
1 tbsp olive oil
1 medium egg white for brushing

Filling
50 g/1.75 oz shelled walnuts
1 garlic clove
1 shallot
1 tbsp butter
2–3 parsley stalks
150 g/5.25 oz ricotta
1 medium egg yolk
2–3 tbsp freshly grated Parmesan
Sea salt
Freshly ground black pepper
Freshly grated nutmeg

Soup
1.2 l/1.25 US quarts vegetable or game stock
20 g/0.7 oz dried forest mushrooms
Salt
4 tbsp Marsala (optional)
Little chive rings as garnish

For the dough, mix flour and salt in a bowl. Add the egg, egg yolks, and olive oil. Coarsely mash with a fork, then knead everything by hand into a smooth dough. Form into a ball, cover in plastic wrap, and chill for at least 30 minutes in the refrigerator.

In the meantime, toast the walnuts for the filling over medium heat in a dry pan golden-brown. Then grind finely (for example, in a mortar). Peel and finely mince the garlic and shallot. Heat the butter in the pan and sauté the garlic and shallot until glossy. Rinse off the parsley, shake dry, and chop finely. Combine everything in a bowl with the ricotta, egg yolk, and parmesan, then stir until smooth. Season with salt, pepper and nutmeg.

For the soup, bring the stock to a boil, add the mushrooms, and let simmer over low heat for 10–15 minutes until they give off enough aroma. Strain the soup through a colander, save the liquid, and put it back into the pot. Season to taste with salt and as much marsala as you like.

Divide the pasta dough into two portions and roll each of them out as thinly as possible, which is easiest to do with a pasta machine. Shape small ravioli out of this: Cut the pasta dough sheets into long strips (about 10 cm/4 inches wide) and place teaspoon-size mounds of the walnut-ricotta cream on them at about 2–3 cm/about 1 inch intervals. Fold the pasta dough over the mounds from the long side, brush with egg white, and fold the other long dough side over it. Press down lightly. Make sure that as little air as possible is enclosed with it. Press firmly with your fingers on the spaces in between, then divide the dough into ravioli with a little pastry wheel or knife.

Boil a large pot of water, add a good amount of salt, and let the ravioli simmer in the lightly boiling water for 5–7 minutes. Remove with a slotted spoon, arrange in the prepared deep dishes, pour the hot soup over them, and garnish with the little chive rings.

TIPSY DUCK BREAST ON ROOT VEGETABLES

This recipe was my very first attempt to prepare a duck breast separated into skin and meat—and it's still one of my favorite recipes. By poaching it, the meat stays wonderfully tender and juicy while the separately fried skin gives it the much-loved crispy effect.

SERVES 4 AS AN APPETIZER
OR 2 AS A MAIN COURSE
PREPARATION TIME: 1 HOUR

Duck Breast

150 g/5.25 oz pearl onions
1 organic orange
1 onion
1/2 l/1.25 US quarts chicken broth
1/2 l/1.25 US quarts strong red wine
2 bay leaves
1 tsp brown sugar
1 tbsp aceto balsamico
1/2 tsp black peppercorns
2 duck breast fillets with skin (200 g/7 oz each)
Sea salt
Freshly ground black pepper
1 tbsp cold butter

Root Vegetables

1 large carrot
1 leek
2 tbsp butter
1 pinch of sea salt

For the duck breast, peel the pearl onions and wash the orange in hot water, then cut it into finger-thick slices. Peel and halve the onion. Sauté cut side down in a large pot over high heat in a dry pan without fat until the first dark spots appear. Pour in the broth and the wine. Add the pearl onions, orange slices, bay leaves, sugar, balsamico, and peppercorns. Bring everything to a boil and simmer over medium heat for about 10 minutes.

In the meantime, prepare the duck breast: Wash fillets, dab dry, and remove the rest of the quills with tweezers, if necessary. Carefully remove the skin. You might need a knife to do this (but don't cut into the meat). Cut the skin into finger-thick strips, then into cubes. Sauté in a pan over medium heat until golden-brown and crisp. Let the duck crackling drain on paper towels.

Reduce the heat of the red-wine broth so that it stops boiling. Add the duck breast fillets and simmer below boiling point in 8–10 minutes. Take out, wrap in aluminum foil, and let rest for a short while. Strain the red-wine broth through a colander (if you like, you can serve the pearl onions with the meal) and set aside. Take about 300 ml/ 10 fl oz and cook over high heat in a small pot until it is reduced to half its volume. Then season the sauce to taste with salt and pepper and stir in the little pieces of butter.

For the vegetables, peel the carrot, cut in half lengthwise, and cut each piece lengthwise into thin slices. Place the slices on top of each other and cut into thin strips. Cut off the root end and green top of the leek. Wash the leek, halve lengthwise, and clean under cold running water. Then cut into pieces about the length of a finger and cut these lengthwise into fine strips. Melt the butter in a pot and brown the vegetables over low to medium heat for 5–8 minutes so that they still have some bite. Season to taste with salt and keep warm.

Cut the duck breast fillets into thin slices and briefly add to the sauce. Then arrange together with the root vegetables and the crisp duck crackling. Even tastes good lukewarm.

SAFFRON POTATO SOUP WITH GINGER PRAWNS

Certain recipes practically beg you to vary them time and again. Potato soup is one of these. My mom's soup was a legend beyond compare and she still makes several pots of it at a time so that everyone can eat their fill. I also wouldn't want to do without my modern variation with curry and bacon. But how about giving the tuber a really classy look for a change? It reaches the table as a sunny yellow temptation with prawns tossed in ginger butter. You will lick your fingers with relish when you've had these.

SERVES 4
PREPARATION TIME: 30 MINUTES

Soup
2 shallots
1/2 large red chili pepper
1 large carrot
3 mealy boiling potatoes
(about 600 g/1.3 lb)
2 tbsp clarified butter
1 l/1 US quart vegetable broth
1/2 tsp saffron threads
200 g/7 oz whipping cream
Sea salt
Freshly ground black pepper

Prawns
12 unpeeled, raw prawns
1 piece of fresh ginger (about 3 cm/ 1.25 inch)
3 tbsp butter
1 pinch salt
4 bamboo skewers

To Taste
Saffron threads for garnishing
Crème fraîche
Baguette

For the soup, peel the shallots and dice finely. Wash the chili pepper, remove the stem, and chop finely. Wash the carrot and cut into thick slices. Peel, wash, and cut the potatoes into large cubes.

Heat the clarified butter in a large pot and sauté the shallot in it until glossy. Add the chili, carrot slices, and potato cubes. Pour in the broth and sprinkle the saffron threads over it. Cover and simmer over medium heat for 15–20 minutes until the vegetables can be easily mashed with a fork. Then mix with the hand-held blender until creamy, add the whipping cream, and season the soup to taste with salt and pepper.

In the meantime, peel the prawns except for the end piece of the tail. Devein them by slightly cutting into the backs lengthwise and pulling out the dark intestinal tract. Then briefly rinse the prawns under cold running water and let them drain on paper towels.

Peel the ginger and chop finely. Let the butter foam in a pan and mix in the ginger. Add the prawns and fry until pink over medium heat for about 1–2 minutes, depending on size. Season with salt. Put 3 ginger prawns on each of the skewers.

Arrange the ginger-prawn skewers with the hot soup. Garnish according to taste with a few saffron threads, as well as crème fraîche. Serve with a baguette.

BASIL GNOCCHI WITH PINE NUT BUTTER

I will frankly admit it—I love potatoes. Even as a child, I liked to pounce on the side dishes like potato dumplings and fried potatoes, sometimes ignoring a great roast. This is why homemade gnocchi are heaven on earth for me. They really can't be compared with those you buy at the store. Once you get the hang of it with the right consistency, they will become your favorite meal.

SERVES 4
PREPARATION TIME: 45 MINUTES
PLUS 1 HOUR COOKING TIME

Gnocchi

1 kg/2.2 lb mealy boiling potatoes
1 handful basil leaves
1 medium egg
1 medium egg yolk
At least 1/2 tsp sea salt
Freshly grated nutmeg
75–125 g/2.75–4.5 oz flour
Plus extra flour for forming (semolina can also be used)

Butter

5–6 tbsp pine nuts
125 g/4.5 oz butter
1 pinch of sea salt

Preheat oven to 200°C/390°F. Wash the potatoes, poke holes in them with a knife and place on a rack in the oven (middle, convection oven 180°C/355°F). Turn over once as they bake for about 1 hour until soft. Peel the potatoes hot and press through a potato ricer into a bowl. Measure 750–800 g/1.65–1.75 lb of them and let them steam for 5 minutes. In the meantime, tear the basil leaves into small pieces and use the hand-held blender to purée with the egg yolk until smooth.

Sprinkle the salt and nutmeg over the potatoes, pour the flour-and-basil egg mixture over them, and combine loosely with a fork. Now you need your hands! Gnocchi dough can be very temperamental because the quality of the potatoes and their water content sometimes demands more, sometimes less flour. But you should always keep these two things in mind: The less flour you use, the lighter and more velvety (but also more fragile!) the gnocchi will become—depending on the potatoes, 10–20% of the amount of potatoes is required. Too much flour makes them as tough as rubber balls. And: You hardly need to knead the gnocchi dough. Just make sure that the dough ingredients are evenly distributed. So gently press the dough together with your hands instead of vigorously kneading it. When the dough is ready, it should be used right away because it will quickly become mushy and moist.

Dust your hands with flour and take small portions of the dough. On a floured countertop, form them into long, thumb-thick logs and cut into pieces about 2 cm/ 0.75 inch in length. Use your thumb to roll each piece down the fork tines or a gnocchi board (Rigagnocchi) so that one side has an indentation and the other has the typical grooved pattern. It may look difficult at the start, but it gets easier with each gnoccho. Place them on a floured sheet.

Boil a large pot of water and generously add salt, then turn down the heat. Carefully let the gnocchi glide into the water and then simmer them over low heat. As soon as they rise to the surface, you can take them out with a slotted spoon. Serve with pine nut butter.

Pine nut butter: Finely chop the pine nuts or grind in a mortar. Foam butter in a pan and add the pine nuts and salt. Fry until golden-brown over a low to medium heat—this often happens faster than you think! Spoon the butter over the gnocchi.

PEPPERED ROAST BEEF WITH SPRING DRESSING

It's really a good idea to buy only the very best beef for this recipe. The meat should be hung for at least three weeks - four is even better, which is a matter of course for any good butcher. My meat thermometer has been a valuable tool in the preparation of this recipe—it's very reliable and prevents overcooking the juicy roast beef meaning it would lose its pink core and become dry. This is a good recipe for a Sunday meal or the brunch buffet—not to mention the sumptuous sandwiches that you can conjure up from the leftovers!

SERVES 4 AS AN ENTRÉE PLUS A HANDFUL OF SANDWICHES
PREPARATION TIME: 30 MINUTES PLUS 1 HOUR AT ROOM TEMPERATURE AND 2–2 1/2 HOURS COOKING TIME

Roast beef

1 kg/2.2 lb well-hung roast beef
2–3 tbsp black peppercorns
1 tsp sea salt
2 tbsp clarified butter

Dressing

1 spring onion
4 radishes
1 shallot
8 tbsp olive oil
1 tbsp white wine vinegar
Sea salt

Plus

Kitchen yarn
Meat thermometer

Take the meat out of the refrigerator 1 hour before roasting and let it come to room temperature. Preheat the oven to 100°C/210°F (convection oven not recommended). Firmly tie the roast beef with kitchen yarn. Coarsely grind the peppercorns in the mortar, mix with sea salt, and rub mixture into the meat on all sides. Let the clarified butter melt in a pan on the stove and briefly fry to seal the roast beef from all sides over high heat until the meat has a nice brown crust.

To be very sure that the roast beef keeps a pale pink core, you can also use a meat thermometer. This can be purchased for a reasonable price in specialized kitchen stores or online. Stick the measuring probe of the thermometer into the meat from above. Its tip should always be at the center of the roast beef so that it shows the core temperature of the meat.

Place the meat in an ovenproof dish with the fat layer facing up, put into the oven (middle rack) and roast for 2–2 1/2 hours. If you would like your roast beef to be the classic pink, the necessary core temperature will be about 60°C/140°F (it stays rare below 55°C/130°F and well-done over 65°C/150°F). As soon as the desired core temperature has been reached, take the roast beef out of the oven, wrap in aluminum foil, and let it stand before cutting. It's best to serve the meat lukewarm or cold with the dressing. Potatoes of all kinds are a good accompaniment: roasted, baked, etc.

Dressing: Wash the spring onion and cut off plenty of the root and green ends. Slice the onion lengthwise into quarters and chop into small pieces. Wash the radishes, clean, and dice finely. Peel the shallot and also dice finely. Mix everything with the olive oil and white wine vinegar, then season to taste with salt. Sprinkle over the thinly sliced roast beef.

Tipp: : If you pack it in foil, the leftover roast beef will keep for a few days in the refrigerator. For a luxurious snack, this makes a perfect sandwich together with ingredients like arugula, tomatoes, avocado, cheese, and a honey-mustard sauce.

DICED RISOTTO WITH LAMB SKEWERS

The special thing about this risotto are the gently sautéed vegetable cubes that—in the best-case scenario and with the necessary skill—are not much larger than the rice grains themselves. This creates a unique taste experience that is only surpassed by the tender pieces of lamb fillet.

SERVES 4
PREPARATION TIME: 45 MINUTES

Risotto

1 large zucchini
1 large eggplant
4 tbsp butter
Sea salt
Freshly ground black pepper
Freshly grated nutmeg
2 shallots
400 g/14 oz risotto rice (for example: Arborio)
250 ml/ 8.5 fl oz dry white wine
About 1 l/1 US quart of hot vegetable stock (you can also use vegetable broth)
50 g/1.75 oz freshly grated Pecorino

Skewers

4 rosemary sprigs
200 g/7 oz lamb fillet
2 tbsp olive oil
Sea salt
Freshly ground black pepper

For the risotto, wash and clean the zucchini and the eggplant. Dice as finely as possible. Let 2 tbsp butter foam in a large pan and lightly sauté the vegetable cubes in it over medium heat for 5–8 minutes. Season to taste with salt, pepper, and nutmeg. Then set aside.

In the meantime, prepare the lamb skewers: The rosemary sprigs are used as skewers - so wash the sprigs, shake dry, and strip off the needles going against the grain. Leave just a few needles at the tip of the sprig. Use a knife to sharpen the thick end of the sprig so that it's easier to skewer the meat. Cut the lamb fillet into 2-cm/0.75-inch cubes and stick them on the rosemary sprigs.

Peel the shallots and dice finely. Melt the rest of the butter in a large pot and sauté the shallots in it until glossy, then add the rice. While stirring over medium heat, brown until the rice grains are also glossy, then pour in the white wine. Now simmer the rice for 20–25 minutes until soft. Keep adding the vegetable stock and (very important!) stir at regular intervals so that the risotto doesn't stick to the bottom of the pot. One or two minutes before the rice is done, add the sliced vegetables. Then stir in the Pecorino and season the risotto to taste with pepper and salt (if necessary).

Near the end of the cooking time, heat the olive oil in a pan. Salt and pepper the lamb skewers and brown in the oil over medium to high heat on each side for a maximum of 1 minute. They should still be slightly pink at the core. Dish out the risotto onto the plates and arrange with the lamb-fillet skewers.

FENNEL-ORANGE SALAD WITH SMOKED TROUT

It's no secret that fennel and orange go well together. If the two are additionally ennobled with smoked fish, this colorful salad turns into a real taste revelation. Sweet, sour, hot, spicy, crisp, and soft—every nuance is represented here. And you don't even have to be a fan of anise (I'm not!) to be enthused about this salad.

SERVES 4 AS A LIGHT ENTRÉE
PREPARATION TIME: 25 MINUTES
PLUS 1 HOUR MARINATING TIME

- 1 lemon
- 4 oranges
- 2 red onions
- 2 fennel bulbs (with the rich green fronds, of course)
- 5 tbsp olive oil
- 1–2 tbsp anise liqueur (for example: Pernod)
- 1–2 pinches of sugar
- Sea salt
- Freshly ground black pepper
- 2 smoked salmon trout fillets

Squeeze out lemon and 1 orange. Peel the onions and slice or cut as finely as possible—a mandolin (vegetable slicer) is perfect for this task. Wash and clean the fennel bulbs. Cut off the fronds and set aside for later use. Cut the bulbs into quarters and also grate finely. Put the vegetables in a big bowl with the citrus juice, cover, and marinate for at least 1 hour.

Then pour the marinade into a small bowl and mix with the olive oil and anise liqueur. Season to taste with sugar, salt, and pepper. Finely chop the fennel fronds and mix 1–2 tbsp of them into the dressing.

Peel the rest of the oranges so that the white skin is also completely removed. Cut the fruit into thin slices crosswise to the individual fruit segments . Arrange the marinated vegetable shavings on plates. Scatter the orange slices, as well as the fish fillets that you have shred into large pieces with your fingers. Generously pour over the dressing.

FAMILY RECIPES

My neighbor Mathilde holds the plate I had brought her the day before with a piece of cake to sample under my nose: "Well, that tasted good ... For a few seconds, I felt like I was back in my grandmother's kitchen when she was making sweet yeast dumplings."

FAMILY RECIPES

The distant clicking of the garden gate had already announced a visitor when I also heard a voice that was very familiar to me: "Luis'? Luis'?" The front door opened (my grandparents kept the front-door key outside during the day) and a short, stocky person with very curly hair and many dimples entered the kitchen. Aunt Kate, as I called her, was my Grandmother Luise's niece. She lived just one street away and shared her passion for baking. She was carrying a baking sheet with fragrant Zwetschgendatschi (damson cake) in front of her and had come to get more damsons: "Hello, Nicky. Is Luis' down in the sewing room?" Sewing room was our nickname for Grandma Luise's little dressmaker's workshop in the cellar. If she wasn't in the kitchen or her sewing room, then she could actually just be in the greenhouse. I sent Aunt Kate back outside, but not without catching a warning that was meant for me:

"But the cake has to cool off first before you cut it, right?!"

As long as I can remember, I spent all of my weekends and vacations at my grandparents' house. Their old house full of nooks and crannies and the big orchard were the best adventure playground that anyone could have conjured up. When they picked me up from school on Friday, it was not unusual for us to continue on directly to pick strawberries, deliver preserves to the relatives or pick up what they had baked, or just simply go to the coffee klatch—there was always time for that.

I was the happiest of all, however, when we paid a visit to grandma's brother Josef in the town of Weihern. He had taken over their father's bakery and baked the very best white pretzels that you could imagine. Between huge sacks of flour and tall stacks of baking sheets, there was always something freshly baked to sample and the bakery cats were always happy when you played with them.

When we got back to the house, my grandfather—who looked after the vegetable garden—was expecting us. "Lene was here and brought us something."

It's no wonder that grandma's pantry and the many storage shelves in the cellar never appeared to be empty. There were countless jam preserves, her favorite Armagnac damsons, cold-smoked ham, stacks of vegetable and fruit crates, and at least one freshly baked cake was always on the kitchen board.

Things couldn't have been better in the land of milk and honey. Grandma's cuisine was down-to-earth and hearty. There were many meat-and-potato dishes, but usually just a simple light meal in the evening. And each meal included a fresh salad from the garden. The seasonal cuisine was the most natural thing in the world for her. If the damsons in the garden were ripe, then there were plum dumplings on the menu. If we could hardly pick the apples fast enough and gave them away by the crate, there was apple strudel made of potato dough for lunch, stewed apples with pancakes, and—obviously—apple cake with coffee. But our very favorite time was the late summer when my grandmother went mushroom-hunting almost every day. Fresh porcini, chestnut boleti, and chanterelles were cooked into a soup that made everyone in the family lick their lips.

There were quite a few dishes that filled the seats at my grandparents' dining table very quickly. These included Schoppala (potato noodles) and every type of Sunday roast. The table was pulled out and everyone helped serve the food. Full and happy, we all sat together for a long time after the meal, drank coffee, and talked about the week that had just passed. Even to this day, Grandma's recipes haven't lost any of their magic for me.

GRANDMA LUISE'S SCHOPPALA

Schoppala is a type of southern German potato side dish for which there are probably a dozen different regional names. It's mostly served with some type of roast or cabbage and is similar to Italian gnocchi dough. Since industrially-made finger noodles can now be purchased in every frozen-food section, it's unfortunate that most people think it's too much work to make these little potato noodles at home–but they taste so much better this way.

When my grandpa greeted me with: "Grandma is making Schoppala!," it was never really clear who was happier about it, him or me.

From early childhood on, I had watched Grandma Luise make the "Schoppala piglets" and diligently helped her because it obviously wasn't that easy to give them the perfect shape. Once they were finally sizzling in the pan, my grandfather and I waited impatiently for the first golden-brown noodles. Which we obviously ate with our fingers!

INGREDIENTS

For 4 as a side dish or snack: 750-800 g/1.65–1.75 lb mealy boiling potatoes | 75–100 g/2.75–3.5 oz flour (as needed) | salt | freshly grated nutmeg | 1 large egg | clarified butter for frying.

PREPARATION

Steam (or boil) potatoes until soft, peel as hot as possible, and press through a potato ricer. Then let cool down for at least 15 minutes. Add the flour, salt, nutmeg, and the egg and mix everything lightly with a fork (don't forget to salt according to taste!). Quickly form into a dough dumpling by hand. The less you knead the potato dough, the better.

Immediately continue kneading it (the dough gets sticky otherwise): Take a handful, form on the floured board into rolls that are at least thumb-thick, and cut into pieces of equal size. Flour your hands and cut into finger-thick finger noodles that are 8–10 cm/3–4 inches long and place on a board dusted with flour (or semolina).

Heat the clarified butter in a large pan and sauté the Schoppala over medium heat until golden-brown. Be sure to turn them over several times. They are wonderful as a side dish for any type of game or meat roast, or as a snack by themselves with a bowl of salad, for example.

FRITTERS

Holidays, annual fairs, and big village weddings always had one thing in common for me when I was a child: They had the very best cakes, tortes, and—above all—the most delicious fritters. At the same time, I could never quite believe my grandmother when she said that the Schmalzküchln (fritters, which are also called Kiachln, Schmalznudeln, or Auszogne in German) were actually pulled across the knee in earlier times (which is why they were called Auszogne, which means "drawn out"). It can be done just as well with greased hands, some feeling, and practice!

INGREDIENTS

Makes about 15 pieces: 50 g/1.75 oz butter (plus a little bit more for brushing) | 500 g/1.1 lb flour | 20 g/0.75 oz fresh yeast | 150–200 ml/5–7 fl oz lukewarm milk | 75 g/2.75 oz sugar | 1 pinch of salt | 2 medium eggs | clarified butter for deep-frying | powdered sugar for dusting

PREPARATION

Melt butter over low heat and let cool. Sift flour into a big bowl and make a well in the middle. Crumble the fresh yeast into it and pour in about one-third of the lukewarm milk. Add 1 pinch of sugar. Stir the yeast milk once, dust with some flour, and cover the bowl. Let the sponge rise in a warm and draft-free place for about 20 minutes until bubbles form.

Add the rest of the milk, the remaining sugar, salt, eggs, and butter. Thoroughly knead by hand or in the kitchen processor with the kneading hooks until the dough is shiny and can easily be lifted out of the bowl. Cut out portions with a tablespoon, roll into balls, brush with butter, cover, and let rise for another 15–20 minutes.

Heat the clarified butter in a tall pan (the liquid fat should come at least 8 cm/3 inches up the sides of the pan). The optimal temperature for deep-frying the fritters is 175°C/345°F. If you dip a wooden spoon into the liquid fat, bubbles should appear, and the temperature is just right.

Rub your fingers with butter (it's easier this way) and shape the little cakes. As you do this, carefully pull each portion of dough out thin from the center and form an evenly thick edge. Then carefully put it into the hot fat and immediately scoop the fat over it a few times with a spoon so that it takes on the typical shape.

As soon as the bottom side has turned golden-brown, turn the little cakes over and bake until done. As you do this, be sure that no more fat gets in the center—the little cakes should stay light on the inside. Let drain on paper towels and then dust with powdered sugar.

sweet & irresistible

PEARS IN SAFFRON-VANILLA SYRUP

This is one of my favorite recipes for two different reasons. On the one hand, it has this wonderful sunny color and the marvelous taste of the pears; on the other, two of my favorite aromas are wedded here. Vanilla and saffron have always been some of the most expensive spices—they should only be used in the very best quality to make this a fine luxury dessert. The little investment will pay off double and threefold. Just the syrup alone is in a class by itself.

SERVES 4–6
PREPARATION TIME: 20 MINUTES PLUS UP TO 30 MINUTES SIMMERING AND MARINATING OVERNIGHT

250 g/9 oz sugar
1 vanilla pod
1 lime
About 1/2 tsp saffron threads
6 firm pears

Serve with

Vanilla ice cream (tastes simply divine with the pears)

Bring 600ml/20 fl oz water and the sugar to a boil in a large pot over high heat while stirring occasionally. Then turn the heat down so that the syrup just continues to simmer very gently. Slice the vanilla pod lengthwise. Scrape out the pulp with a knife and add to the sugar syrup together with the pod. Squeeze out the lime and add the juice, as well as the saffron threads.

Either halve or quarter the pears, then core and peel them. Add to the syrup. Cover and let simmer until soft, which could take up to 30 minutes. Carefully turn over the individual pear pieces occasionally by using two spoons. They are done if you no longer feel any resistance when you poke them with the tip of the knife (but they also shouldn't fall apart).

Carefully place the pear pieces in a tall container (canning jars are a good choice for this) and pour the syrup over them until all of the fruit is covered. Let cool, then cover and marinate in the refrigerator for at least one night—only then will they really take on the sunny yellow color of the saffron. The longer you let the pears marinate in the saffron-vanilla syrup, the more distinct their indescribable aroma will be (which is why it's also always worthwhile to prepare a larger batch of them!). Serve the pears with vanilla ice cream and sprinkle with some syrup.

PASSION FRUIT PARFAIT

Parfaits are the perfect desserts. They don't require any witchcraft in terms of their preparation, are easily made in advance, and your guests will be immensely impressed. The little black seeds of the passion fruit and the white meringue crumbs give this parfait an exciting inner life, and the red mulled Bordeaux wine gives it quite a kick. Whether the boss is coming to dinner or you are cooking for your beloved—this is the right dessert for the occasion!

SERVES 4
PREPARATION TIME: 45 MINUTES
PLUS 4 HOURS OF FREEZING

Parfait

1 vanilla pod
3 large egg yolks
50 g/1.75 oz sugar
2 passion fruit
4 tbsp meringue crumbs (about the size of a hazelnut, possibly extra for sprinkling on top)
200 g/7 oz whipping cream

Reduction

400 ml/13.5 fl oz strong red wine (such as Cabernet Sauvignon)
50–75 g/1.75–2.75 oz sugar
1 organic orange
1 piece of fresh ginger (about 1 cm/ 0.5 inch)
1/2 cinnamon stick
1 star anise pod
1–2 tsp cornstarch (if necessary)

Plus

4 ramekins of about 100 ml/ 3.5 oz each

For the parfait, slice the vanilla pod lengthwise, scrape out the pulp with a knife, and put into a large metal bowl together with the egg yolks and the sugar. Whisk over a hot bain-marie—this rarely takes more than 4 minutes, even by hand. The mixture will first be foamy, then creamy. Set the bowl into ice-cold water and keep beating until the egg crème has cooled down. Halve the passion fruit, scoop out the pulp and seeds, and stir into the crème with the meringue crumbs. Beat the whipping cream until stiff. First fold in one-third of it into the crème, then gently fold the rest into it so that it remains fluffy. Fill into the ramekins and freeze for at least 4 hours.

In the meantime, boil the wine and sugar for the reduction in a pan. Wash the orange in hot water and peel 2–3 strips of the zest with the potato peeler and add to the wine. Squeeze out the orange and pour the juice in through a sieve. Peel the ginger, cut into slices, and also add with the cinnamon and anise. Boil everything down to at least half the volume over small to medium heat in 20–30 minutes. If the reduction is still too liquid, stir the cornstarch with 2–3 tbsp of cold water until smooth before mixing it into the reduction, which should now be simmering (!). (The reduction gets even thicker when it cools down, so a bit of intuition is required here). Remove from the stove and let it cool down. The consistency is perfect when the reduction drips from the spoon like runny honey.

Dip the ramekins into hot water for a few seconds before serving. Then run a knife along the edge and loosen the parfait before turning it upside down on the plates. Let it thaw for a few minutes—that's the only way it will develop its full creaminess—and sprinkle with the reduction. If you like, you can also sprinkle a few meringue crumbs on it. By the way, the parfait can be easily kept in the freezer compartment for several days. It's a dessert you can make in advance for special occasions.

GREEN CHOCOLATE MOUSSE

The motto of using only the very best ingredients is a must for this mousse. To make it, I use only chocolate that I also like to enjoy on its own—and a relatively mild olive oil. When I let people sample the mousse for the first time, it's always fun to see how everyone thinks they know what this mysterious ingredient is. Enthused and baffled, they eat spoon after spoon—and then finally ask for the solution to the puzzle. If you would like a stronger flavor, then choose an especially fruity olive oil.

SERVES 4–6
PREPARATION TIME: 45 MINUTES
PLUS 3 HOURS FOR COOLING

Mousse

200 g/7 oz high-quality dark chocolate (50–70% cocoa content)
75 ml/2.5 fl oz very good olive oil
3 large eggs
50 g/1.75 oz raw cane sugar
50 g/1.75 oz granulated sugar
200 g/7 oz whipping cream

Topping

75 g/2.75 oz granulated sugar
5 tbsp pine nuts
1 green apple (Granny Smith)
1 green pear
1 kiwi
1–2 handfuls of green grapes (seedless)

For the mousse, coarsely chop the chocolate or break into pieces. Put into a bowl and slowly melt over the hot bain-marie (the bowl must not touch the water), then stir in the oil. Set aside and let cool for 15 minutes.

For the topping, melt the granulated sugar in a pan over medium heat without stirring. As soon as the last sugar crystals have dissolved and the sugar begins to turn light brown, add the pine nuts and stir in with a heat-resistant spoon (be careful—the sugar is very hot!). Pour onto a silicon baking mat or baking paper, spread into a thin layer, and let it harden. As soon as the crunch has cooled off, break into pieces. Either crush it coarsely in a mixer or place in a freezer bag and crumble with the help of a rolling pin. (The crunch will keep for several days in an air-tight container.)

Back to the chocolate mousse: Separate the eggs. Beat the egg yolks together with the cane sugar (by hand or with the mixer) until the mixture is fluffy and creamy. Using another bowl, beat the egg whites until stiff together with the granulated sugar. In a third bowl, beat the whipping cream. One after the other, carefully stir into the chocolate: first the egg-yolk mixture, then the beaten egg whites, and finally the whipping cream. Fill into pretty ramekins or glasses. Cover and let it become firm in the refrigerator for at least 4 hours.

Shortly before serving, wash the apple and pear because both do not need to be peeled. Quarter and core the apple, then cut into thin wedges and slices. Quarter and core the pear, then cut into fine slices. Peel the kiwi, cut into sixths, and slice into fine chunks. Wash the grapes and either halve or cut into slices, depending on their size (and your time). Mix the fruit, spread over the chocolate mousse, and sprinkle with the pine nut crunch.

TINTO-FUEGO SORBET WITH APEROL

Negroni isn't just a cocktail but also the name of one of the best bars in Munich. It only takes five minutes to walk from our place to our favorite bar, which is sometimes a fateful circumstance because a short meeting with friends often turns into a long night. The two charismatic owners Mauro and Michele are true masters of their trade. When they aren't holding seminars or jetting around the globe for international championships, they mix unique cocktails for each of the guests and tailor them completely to their individual wishes. In addition to their legendary Russian Satellite, I love the fruity, deep-red Tinto Fuego—so much that it became my inspiration for this sorbet.

SERVES 4–6
PREPARATION TIME: 20 MINUTES PLUS 30 MINUTES FOR COOLING, AS WELL AS THE FREEZING TIME

150 g/5.25 oz raw cane sugar
2 organic limes
300 g/10.5 oz fresh strawberries (defrosted frozen berries also work well)
100 ml/ 3.5 fl oz Aperol (Italian bitter aperitif or Campari as a substitute) plus extra for sprinkling

Decoration

A few basil leaves
2–3 tbsp granulated sugar
Aperol for moistening

Boil 125 ml/4.25 fl oz water and cane sugar. Stir occasionally until all of the sugar crystals have dissolved, then take the syrup from the stove. Wash the lime with hot water and grate the zest finely into the syrup. Squeeze out the lime juice and add to the mixture. Let the syrup steep, then allow it to cool off for at least 30 minutes. Next, wash the strawberries, remove the stalks, and cut into small pieces. Purée the berries and strain the puree through a fine sieve (the sorbet really melts on the tongue without the small seeds). Also pour the cooled sugar syrup through a sieve to remove the lime zest. Then stir the Aperol and the strawberry puree into it. Now let the puree turn into sorbet. There are two ways to do this.

1. With an ice-cream maker: Cover and chill the puree well in the refrigerator (for at least 1 hour), then let it freeze in the ice-cream maker according to manufacturer's directions.
2. Without an ice-cream maker: It's best to pour the puree into a wide, flat container, cover, and place in the freezer until it has turned into a sorbet. This takes about 5 hours. Stir with a fork once an hour to crush the ice crystals that develop. The frozen sorbet becomes extra creamy if you use the hand blender before the very last freezing phase.

If you like to serve sorbet in beautiful glasses, it's best to do it in style with a decorative sugar rim: Grind the basil leaves with the sugar into a fine paste in the mortar and shake onto a flat plate. Moisten the edges of the glass with a finger dipped in Aperol and press into the herb sugar. Then carefully fill each of the glasses with 1 scoop of sorbet and sprinkle with some Aperol.

KAISERSCHMARRN

When someone asks Oliver and me about our favorite sweet dish, we answer in chorus "Kaiserschmarrn" (Emperor's pancake)! Even though some of the Bavarian inns serve up a wonderful Kaiserschmarrn, it still tastes best when made at home. After a lot of experimenting, we finally found "our recipe." The Kaiserschmarrn is prepared on the stove only and isn't put in the oven (which makes it a bit denser). At the end, it's caramelized to a golden-brown color with a generous helping of butter and powdered sugar over a good amount of heat. Be sure not to skimp on the butter and sugar because that would be a crime! There's just one point that we can't agree on: with or without raisins?

SERVES 2–3 AS SWEET ENTREE OR
4 AS DESSERT
PREPARATION TIME: 20 MINUTES
PLUS 30 MINUTES EXPANSION AND
POSSIBLY SOAKING TIME

- 50 g/1.75 oz raisins (optional)
- 50 ml/1.75 fl oz rum (optional)
- 4–5 large eggs
- 1 vanilla pod
- 250 ml/8.5 fl oz milk
- 2 tbsp sugar
- 150 g/5.25 oz flour
- 1 pinch of salt
- 75–100 g/2.75–3.5 oz butter
- 50 g/1.75 oz almond slivers
- 3 tbsp powdered sugar (plus extra for sprinkling)

Serve with

Plum compote or applesauce

If adding raisins to the Kaiserschmarrn, first let them soak in rum for 30 minutes and drain them in a sieve.

Separate the eggs. Slice the vanilla pod lengthwise, scrape out the pulp, and mix with the milk, egg yolks, 1 tbsp sugar, flour, and salt to make a smooth batter (it's best to do this by hand) and let expand for about 30 minutes. Then beat the egg whites with the remaining sugar until stiff and gently fold into the batter.

Melt half of the butter over medium heat in a large pan (it's best to use a non-stick pan). Pour in the batter and smooth it out. If you soaked the raisins, sprinkle them over the batter. Bake until the bottom side is golden-brown (don't let it get too dark!).

Then tear this thick pancake with two wooden spoons into bite-sized pieces. Sprinkle the almond slivers over it, distribute the rest of the butter between the pieces of Kaiserschmarrn, and generously dust everything with powdered sugar. Keep turning the pieces and fry from all sides until golden-brown over high heat until the sugar is caramelized and the almonds are crisp.

Immediately serve the Kaiserschmarrn with plum compote or applesauce—dust with powdered sugar and it's ready!

SEMIFREDDO WITH PUMPKIN-SEED CRUNCH

Of all of the homemade desserts, this semifreddo is one of my absolute favorites. Easy to prepare. Cold and creamy. Nutty and crispy! Simply irresistible!!! If you are annoyed by the pumpkin-seed oil in the ingredient list—just try it out because you'll find it creates a sensational taste experience.

SERVES 4
PREPARATION TIME: 30 MINUTES
PLUS 4 HOURS FOR FREEZING

60 g/2 oz pumpkin seeds
40 g/1.5 oz white sugar
4 large egg yolks
50 g/1.75 oz raw cane sugar
1 tbsp cognac
2 tbsp pumpkin-seed oil
200 g/7 oz whipping cream

Plus
4 ramekins of about 100 ml/3.5 fl oz each

Toast the pumpkin seeds in a dry pan over medium heat until they begin to crackle and slightly change color. Take them out of the pan. Put the granulated sugar in the pan and let it melt without stirring. As soon as the last sugar crystals have dissolved and the sugar begins to turn light brown, stir in the pumpkin seeds with a heat-resistant spoon until they are evenly coated with caramel (be careful—the sugar gets very hot!). Pour onto a silicon baking mat or baking paper, spread into a thin layer, and let it harden. As soon as the crunch has cooled off, break it into coarse pieces (set a few aside for garnish). Put it into a freezer bag and break into a relatively fine crunch with the help of the rolling pin or even a heavy pan.

Combine egg yolks, cane sugar, cognac, and oil in a metal bowl. Whisk over a hot bain-marie. Even by hand, this rarely takes more than 4 minutes. The mixture first becomes foamy, then creamy. Set the bowl in ice-cold water and keep beating until the egg crème is cold and has become slightly thickened. Now stir in the 50 g/1.75 oz of pumpkin seeds.

Beat the whipping cream until stiff. First carefully fold one-third, and then the rest, into the crunch crème. It should still be nice and airy. Fill the mixture in the ramekins and place in the freezer for at least 4 hours.

Immerse the ramekins in hot water for a few seconds before serving, then slide a knife along the edge and loosen the semifreddo before you turn it upside down on the plates. Let it defrost for a few minutes. Sprinkle with the rest of the crunch and serve.

COFFEE POWER

Next to tiramisu, which is often much too rich, the Italian panna cotta is the export hit among the desserts. Its inexhaustible versatility makes it one of my sweet favorites. The "cooked whipping cream" can be wonderfully infused with all kinds of aromas ranging from fruit of the season to exotic spices or fresh herbs. Through the addition of freshly roasted coffee beans, this panna cotta almost turns into a large mug of latte—at least in terms of the taste. To top it off, it almost eliminates the need for the obligatory espresso after the meal.

When I—as in this recipe—want to serve the panna cotta in pretty ramekins instead of turning them upside down on a plate, I use as little gelatin as possible and am rewarded with a smooth melt-in-your-mouth consistency. By the way, I think it's part of the characteristic look of a panna cotta when the vanilla pulp sinks to the bottom. But this can easily be avoided by letting the prepared whipping-cream mixture gel (be sure to stir every once in a while) until the little black seeds no longer sink to the bottom and then distribute it into the molds.

SERVES 4
PREPARATION TIME: 30 MINUTES
PLUS 5 HOURS FOR COOLING

500 g/1.1 lb whipping cream
50 g/1.75 oz raw cane sugar
1 vanilla pod
3 tsp coffee beans
2 1/2 sheets of clear gelatin
100 ml/3.5 fl oz coffee liqueur (such as Kahlua)

Heat the whipping cream and sugar in a pot. Slice the vanilla pod lengthwise, scrape out the pulp out with a knife, and put into the whipping cream together with the pod. Coarsely grind the coffee beans in a mortar and add to the mixture. Now let the whipping cream simmer gently for about 10 minutes, stirring occasionally. In the meantime, soak 2 sheets of gelatin in a bowl of cold water.

Then remove the pot from the stove, pour the whipping cream through a fine sieve and set aside. Squeeze the water from the softened sheets of gelatin and carefully stir into the hot whipping cream until they are completely dissolved. Fill mixture into small glasses or individual bowls. Cover and let become firm in the refrigerator.

After about 3 hours, the panna cotta will already be solid enough to prepare the jelly layer: Soak the rest of the gelatin in cold water and then heat the Kahlua in a small pot (but don't let it boil). Squeeze the water out of the gelatin and dissolve in the liqueur by stirring. Let the liqueur cool off for 10 minutes, then carefully distribute onto the panna cotta with a tablespoon. Cover and keep cold in the refrigerator for at least 2 more hours.

CLOUD NINE

This curd-cheese mousse is the perfect summer dessert. It's light and airy and very easy to prepare. You can give it a new look each time with fresh, seasonal fruit. Mail from some of my readers made me realize that although curd cheese can be found in any refrigerated section in Germany, it is difficult to find it in places like the USA. So what to do? A few days later, I was able to make a mousse that was just as creamy without the curd cheese—creamy Greek yogurt made from cow's milk is the perfect substitute!

SERVES 4
PREPARATION TIME: 15 MINUTES
PLUS 6 HOURS OF COOLING
(OVERNIGHT IS EVEN BETTER)

Mousse

1 vanilla pod
1 organic lemon
500 g/1.1 lb curd cheese (40% fat is good, but it should be at least 20%; use Greek yogurt as a substitute)
50 g/1.75 oz sugar
200 g/7 oz whipping cream

Serve with

Fresh fruit
Grated chocolate

Plus

Gauze bandage (from the pharmacy)
Cœur-à-la-crème molds or a large sieve

For the mousse, slice the vanilla pod lengthwise, scrape out the pulp with a knife, and put into a large bowl. Wash the lemon in hot water, finely grate the zest, and combine with the curd cheese and sugar in a bowl. Mix everything vigorously until the sugar crystals have dissolved.

Beat the whipping cream until stiff in a second bowl and fold into the curd-cheese mixture. Line the individual dessert molds for cœur à la crème (porcelain molds with small holes in the bottom) or a large sieve evenly with strips of gauze bandage and fill with the curd-cheese mixture. Smooth out. Cover and place in the refrigerator for at least 6 hours—overnight is even better. Let the excessive liquid drain. (It's best to hang the sieve in a large bowl or place the small molds in an ovenproof dish so that it catches the liquid.)

Then turn the small molds upside down directly onto the plates and carefully remove the gauze bandage. If you prepared the curd-cheese mousse in a large sieve, turn it upside down onto a wooden cutting board and then cut off individual pieces from the mousse with a tablespoon. Serve with fresh fruit and grated chocolate.

Variation: For a colorful and especially fruity curd-cheese mousse, add 100–150 g/3.5–5.25 oz of fresh fruit purée (such as raspberries or strawberries) directly to the curd-cheese mixture (before you fold in the whipping cream). You may need a bit more sugar as a result. Just adapt the mousse to your own taste..

QUICK COCONUT ICE CREAM WITH SAFFRON

I ate a similar ice cream years ago on one of the small Maledive islands and was hooked on it from the first spoon. What I erroneously thought was mango ice cream tasted like fresh coconuts and contained red saffron threads that were responsible for its brilliant yellow color and only became visible when spooning it. Once I was home again, I immediately started experimenting. The result was a quick coconut ice cream that is the perfect finish for any Asian menu and always creates a vacation mood.

SERVES 3–4 (DEPENDING ON HOW HUNGRY THEY ARE FOR ICE CREAM)
PREPARATION TIME: 15 MINUTES PLUS FREEZING TIME

200 g/7 oz whipping cream
300 ml/10 fl oz coconut milk
75–100 g/2.75 to 3.5 oz sugar
1/2 tsp saffron threads

Serve with

Exotic fruit like pineapple, lychees, and passion fruit (cut as small as you like)
Coconut chips

Combine the whipping cream in a pot with the coconut milk. Add the sugar and the saffron threads, and bring the mixture to a boil. Simmer gently over low heat for about 10 minutes, stirring now and then. Remove from the stove and let cool. Then turn the coconut-saffron whipping cream into ice cream. There are two ways to do this:

1. With an ice-cream maker: Cover the coconut-saffron whipping cream and chill first in the refrigerator (at least 1 hour), then let it freeze in the ice-cream maker according to manufacturer's directions.
2. Without an ice-cream maker: It's best to pour the coconut-saffron whipping cream into a wide, flat container, cover, and place in the freezer. After 1 hour, take out of the freezer and either stir well with a whisk or the hand blender to crush the ice crystals that develop. Then put it back into the freezer and repeat the procedure every hour until the ice cream is creamy and has reached the desired firmness. (This basically works for all types of ice cream, but the results are much more satisfactory for sorbets than for the dairy ice cream.)

To serve the ice cream, scoop it into glasses or little bowls. Garnish as desired with exotic fruit and/or coconut chips.

DELICIOUSLY CRUNCHY HAZELNUT WAFERS

I believe that a fine dessert is the most important course of a good meal. As the last dish, it's the one that we remember the most. But, above all, it has the exclusive mission of tantalizing our palate—the hunger has already been satiated at this point in time. Yet, there are people who voluntarily abstain from dessert and prefer to have a good cheese platter. If you serve the home-baked, very delicate hazelnut wafers, you can even make both sides happy.

SERVES 6–8 AS A SNACK
WITH A CHEESE PLATTER
PREPARATION TIME: 20 MINUTES
PLUS ABOUT 14–16 MINUTES
FOR BAKING

100 g/3.5 oz shelled hazelnuts
50 g/1.75 oz sugar
1/4 tsp fine sea salt
20 g/0.75 oz flour
3 large egg whites

Preheat the oven to 175°C/345°F (convection oven 160°C/320°F). Toast the nuts in a dry pan over medium heat until they have a few dark spots on them. Move the hazelnuts onto a dish towel and let cool briefly. Then vigorously rub them with the towel until (almost) all of the skin has peeled off. Put the peeled nuts into the electric grinder and coarsely chop. Take out about one-fifth of them and set them aside for later, then finely grind the rest.

Mix the ground nuts with sugar, salt, and flour in a bowl. Briefly beat the egg white with a fork in a separate bowl so that it starts to be foamy (but not stiff yet) and stir into the nut mixture.

Cover a baking sheet with a silicon baking mat or with baking paper. Spread the hazelnut mixture onto the sheet: For an even shape, you can use cookie cutters and fill them as thinly as possible with the batter. But you can save time by baking a large slab of dough. To do it this way, spread the nut mixture over the entire sheet until it is wafer-thin—this is very easy with a palette knife. Finally, sprinkle the chopped nuts evenly across it.

Put the sheet into the oven (middle). Bake the nut mixture for 14–16 minutes until it develops an even brown color. Then take the sheet out of the oven. Remove the smaller nut wafers with a spatula; turn the large baked slab upside down onto a board and carefully remove the mat or baking paper. Let the hazelnut wafer cool off completely on a kitchen rack; once cool, break the large nut wafers into uneven pieces. Stored in airtight containers, they stay fresh for a few days. Serve with cheese and fresh fruit.

Inspiration – for a cheese platter that goes well with the wafers: some semi-hard cheese (such as Felsenkeller mountain cheese), hard cheese (such as Pecorino), soft cheese (such as Brie de Meaux), blue cheese (such as Gorgonzola), goat cheese (such as Valençay), fresh fruit like physalis, figs, pears, grapes, nuts, and something sweet (such as jam, chutney, or fig mustard).

HILUX
ΙΔ.ΧΡΗΣΗ
ΩΦ. 1180 ΑΠ. 1205
ΜΙΚ.2385
ΕΔΡΑ ΠΡΑΣΙΝΑΔΑ

SUPER
MARKET

BOAT TRIP IN GREECE

Cooking on board was a challenge every single day. With heavy seas and temperatures like a Finnish sauna, it took a lot of skill to put a decent lunch on the table for the hungry crew.

BOAT TRIP IN GREECE

You could hear Ulrike's enthusiasm through the telephone. "Georg and Eri rented a yacht for two weeks this summer to sail the Aegean, and guess what ... I'm going with them!" The words bubbled out of her like a waterfall. After describing all the details of the planned trip, she had a question for me:

"A berth is still free–why don't you guys come along with us?"

Despite all of the arising adversities, we met at the end of July in the south of the Greek peninsula of Sithonia to take over the Sheria from the old crew. We used motorboats to carry the luggage, provisions, and a huge supply of drinking water on board before Georg, our skipper, assigned the berths and explained the boat to us. A little while later, we weighed anchor and left the bay. There were no clouds to be seen. The sky and the sea sparkled like crazy in deep shades of blue and turquoise as the airstream brought the cooling we longed for. There were happy faces wherever you looked. While the music drifting up from the salon alternated between Amy Winehouse and Sergio Mendes, our time on the deck was spent with reading and being on the lookout for dolphins.

And this is how we reached the harbor for the first night after a few hours on the sea. Georg, who knew the area from previous trips, was able to show us the tavern of the little town from the anchoring ground. Because we were so hungry, the Sheria was moored in no time and we were already clinking glasses to our first mutual sailing tour on the terrace of the tavern just a few minutes later. And Georg hadn't promised too much–many dishes with wonderful meze were soon piled on the table. Everyone sampled a bit of everything and we quickly found our favorites, the tzatziki and the strongly seasoned saganaki (baked sheep's cheese) especially appealed to all of us. This was followed by grilled platters with freshly caught fish and dessert on the house–the waiter surprised us with giant platters that were brimming with watermelon chunks. It was already long after nightfall when we returned to the boat, where we sipped the obligatory nightcap in the moonlight.

The first rays of the sun had hardly fallen through the window when the early risers of our eight-person crew crawled out of their berths. A flurry of activity had already started in the harbor, so we set off to look for the only store in the village.

Supermarkets in foreign countries hold a magical fascination for me. They have different smells than our own, the packaging has a different design, and there are always unfamiliar things for me to discover.

The little village supermarket was located at the very end of the harbor and looked like an eccentric mom-and-pop grocery store. I was overjoyed to stock up on mastic gum (resinous gum from pistachio trees) while Ulrike and Oliver raided the shelf with pistachio candy and Sabine took care of the essentials like fresh yogurt, bread, cookies, eggs and fruit. Back on board, everyone tried to squeeze into the tiny kitchen. A little while later, a pan with steaming scrambled eggs and a gigantic bowl of chopped fruit and yoghurt were placed on the table while Georg already raved about our next destination–a lonely bay with crystal-clear water. To get there, we sailed around the second finger of Chalkidiki and were able to admire the impressive silhouette of the sacred Mount Athos. After half a day in a northerly direction, we had reached Vouvourou and our skipper proved to be right: The water of the bay radiated turquoise and not a soul could be seen anywhere. In high spirits, we jumped into the water and everyone agreed that no place in the world could have been more beautiful at that moment.

SHEEP'S CHEESE
BAKED IN FOIL

Since we were able to indulge extensively in Greek cuisine during every shore leave (we couldn't ever get enough of the baked sheep's cheese and authentic Greek salad), we just had a quick and uncomplicated alternative program in our board kitchen: Anyone who has ever fought with a cardan-suspension gas stove in a rocking space of about five square feet at what feels like 50°C/120°F room temperature will always carefully consider what to set in front of the hungry crew. In this case, the magic word is usually pasta—the simpler, the better! But a certain amount of improvisational talent was required here because large pots and pans were in short supply on board the Sheria. The anger of the Italian pasta gods would probably have rained down upon us had they seen how little water we used to get two pounds of noodles to be al dente. At the end of the cooking time, they were already spilling over the edge of the pot—but everyone still thought it tasted absolutely amazing.

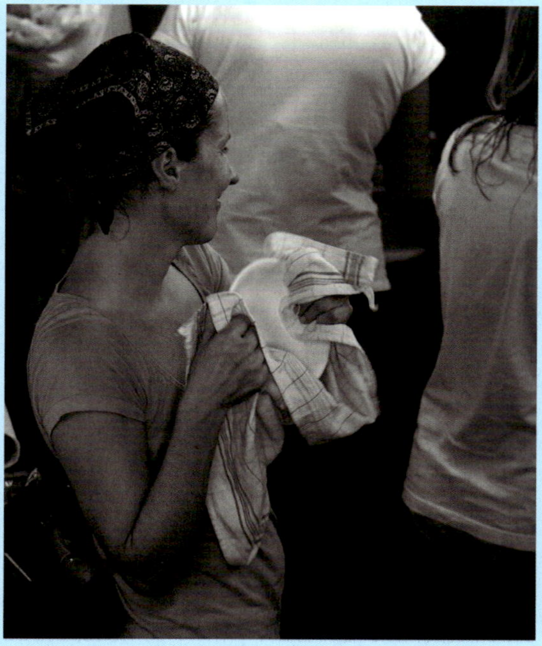

INGREDIENTS

For 4: Aluminum foil | 4 generous finger-thick slices of feta (sheep's cheese) | freshly ground pepper | ground cumin (optional) | oregano (dried or freshly chopped) | 4–6 garlic cloves | 1–2 large, red chili peppers| 2 hot peppers | 100 g/3.5 oz. Kalamata olives | 200 g/7 oz cherry tomatoes (best if they're still on the vine) | olive oil for drizzling | flat bread for dipping

PREPARATION

Preheat the stove to 200°C/390°F (convection oven 180°C/355°F). Cut a piece of the aluminum foil for each serving (at least 30 x 30 cm/12 x 12 inches).

Place 1 slice of feta at the center of each aluminum-foil square. Season with pepper, cumin, and oregano. Peel the garlic cloves (remove the green shoot), finely mince, and spread over the feta. Wash the chilies and hot peppers, remove the stems, and finely chop or cut into rings, with or without seeds (it's hotter with), depending on the desired degree of hotness, and also distribute over the feta. Add the olives and put 1 small vine of tomatoes on each piece of cheese. Then drizzle with a generous shot of oil.

Now loosely wrap the aluminum foil around everything and fold it into an airtight little package. Bake on a sheet in the middle of the oven for about 20 minutes. The feta will have absorbed the various aromas and be wonderfully soft by then. Be sure to dip the flat bread into the splendidly spicy olive oil-feta drippings!

YOGURT WITH HONEY AND ROASTED NUTS

Ever since we live across the street from a Greek greengrocer in Munich, we have become hooked on full-fat Greek yogurt. It has an undisputed number-one spot at the top of my list of yogurts because of its especially mild taste and extra creaminess. Sometimes I even eat the variety made of goat's milk. With some strong honey and a handful of nuts, it makes a quick breakfast highlight.

INGREDIENTS

For 4: 100g/3.5 oz mixed nuts (walnuts, pine nuts, almonds, hazelnuts, pistachios, pumpkin seeds) | 600 g/1.3 lb full-fat Greek yogurt | 8 tbsp fluid honey

PREPARATION

Coarsely chop the large nuts, then briefly toast the nut mixture in a dry pan at medium heat. Stir the yogurt, pour into little bowls (or recycled yogurt glasses) and sprinkle the honey and nuts over it.

GREEK SALAD

Even the simplest dishes just taste better when you're on vacation. Maybe it's because of all the new impressions, and it's easier to enjoy things without the stress of everyday life. The available fresh ingredients are also very important. If you want to prepare a truly authentic Greek Salad, then the tastiest tomatoes are just good enough. If you have a Greek deli in your neighborhood, be sure to sample the feta and olives there.

INGREDIENTS

For 4: 1 large salad cucumber | 1 large, red onion | 3–4 Roma tomatoes | 250 g/9 oz feta (sheep's cheese) | 100 g/3.5 oz Kalamata olives | dressing: sea salt, freshly ground black pepper, a generous amount of the best olive oil, and white wine vinegar, dried oregano (optional) | flat bread

PREPARATION

Peel the cucumbers, halve lengthwise, and cut crosswise into thick slices. Peel the onion, halve, and cut into thicker slices. Wash the tomatoes and cut into thick slices or coarse chunks. Be sure to remove the stem base. Cut the feta into large cubes or break it into pieces. Arrange the prepared ingredients in salad bowls and garnish with the olives.

Add the dressing to the salad just before serving—with sea salt (be careful how much you use because the feta is already quite salty), pepper, olive oil, and the white wine vinegar plus oregano (optional). Serve with the flat bread.

healthy & happy

TWO KINDS OF LASSI

Lassi, the easily digestible yogurt drink that is primarily served in Indian restaurants, relieves not only the spiciness of Asian dishes—it is also excellent as a breakfast companion or refreshment between meals. In addition to the classic mango lassi, there are countless variations that are worth trying.

Whenever I cook a really spicy curry, there is always at least one large pitcher of lassi next to it on the table—serving as a personal fire extinguisher for the more sensitive palates of some of our guests.

EACH RECIPE SERVES 4
PREPARATION TIME:
10 MINUTES EACH

Flower Lassi

1 vanilla pod
3 green cardamom pods
600 g/1.3 lb oz natural yogurt
5 tbsp sugar (or more according to taste)
3–5 ice cubes
5 tbsp elderflower syrup (or more according to taste)

Tangerine Lassi

6–8 tangerines
600 g/1.3 lb natural yogurt
5 tbsp sugar (or more according to taste)
3–5 ice cubes

Flower Lassi:
Slice the vanilla pod lengthwise and scrape out the pulp with a small knife. Break open the cardamom pods, remove the small black seeds and finely grind them in a mortar.

Mix the vanilla pulp and ground cardamom in a blender with natural yogurt, sugar, 300 ml/10 fl oz cold water (you can also use still mineral water), ice cubes, and the elderflower syrup until frothy. Taste and add sugar, as needed. Fill into glasses and immediately serve cold.

Tangerine Lassi:
Halve and squeeze out the tangerines so that they make 300 ml of juice. Mix with the natural yogurt, sugar, and ice cubes until frothy in the blender. Taste and add sugar, as needed. Fill into glasses and immediately serve cold.

EGGS IN A GLASS

are nothing more than breakfast eggs that come to the table already peeled in a glass. A tasty topping is what turns them into something very special. The peeling requires the right feeling so that a) you don't burn your fingers and b) you won't injure the wobbly-soft egg—which also happens to me once in a while. Unfortunately, the freshest eggs, which are best suited for this recipe, are the hardest to take out of the shell—rinsing them with cold water tends to spare the fingers, but does not make it easier to peel the eggs. However: It's worth the effort! And the peeled egg can be topped with a variety of ingredients—ranging from Asiatic to spicy to elegant. But my personal favorite, migas con chorizo, can hardly be beat...

SERVES 1
PREPARATION TIME:
10–20 MINUTES EACH

Topping: Migas con Chorizo

1/2 small slice of rye-wheat bread (from the previous day, white bread is also good)
1 piece of chorizo (2–3 cm/about 1 inch)
1 tsp of olive oil
Medium spicy, smoked paprika powder (Pimentón de la Vera) or cayenne pepper

or

Topping: Toast with Lobster Butter

1 slice toast bread
1 tsp lobster butter (deli)
1 tsp trout caviar

plus

Base, Decoration, Spice

1 very fresh organic medium egg
Garden cress as garnish
Sea salt

Toppingsj

Either finely dice the bread and chorizo for migas con chorizo. Heat the olive oil in a pan and sauté the cubes over medium heat for a few minutes until they are crisp. Sprinkle a little smoked paprika powder or cayenne pepper over it.

Or cut the bread into finger-thick slices for toast with lobster butter. Melt the butter in a pan, then fry the toast slices over medium heat on both sides until crisp.

Base

Bring plenty of water to a boil in a pot. Prick the egg on the bottom and carefully let it slide into the boiling water with the help of a tablespoon. Cook egg either soft as butter (5–6 minutes) or almost hard (7–8 minutes) according to your own taste.

Then remove the egg from the pot with the tablespoon and rinse under cold running water. Now you need clean hands and just the right touch: Very lightly tap all sides of the egg on the countertop so that the peel has cracks and then peel it (don't despair if the results aren't perfect for the first egg!).

Finish

Place the egg in a glass while trying to keep it as intact as possible and add the selected topping. For the toast with lobster butter, don't forget the trout caviar. Garnish everything with the garden cress and serve immediately. Serve with sea salt for seasoning at the table.

LEMON COUSCOUS WITH CURRY VEGETABLES

Even beyond tabbouleh, couscous can be transformed into many exciting salad variations that are tantalizing both warm and cold. My favorite mixture of crunchy curry vegetables and lemony couscous makes friends quickly at any brunch or picnic. And even when I intend to prepare an extra batch of it each time so that I can sink my teeth into the leftovers the next day, there is never—I swear—a crumb of couscous that remains for later.

SERVES 4
PREPARATION TIME: 30 MINUTES

2 small onions
1 carrot
1 zucchini
12 spears of green asparagus
2 scallions
1/2 large red chili pepper
2 organic lemons
300 g/10.5 oz instant couscous
Sea salt
2 tbsp olive oil (plus extra for seasoning to taste)
3–4 tbsp pine nuts
Freshly ground black pepper
1 tsp sugar
1 tsp curry powder
Cayenne pepper (optional)
4 tbsp Greek natural yogurt or sour cream

Prepare the vegetables: peel, halve, and cut the onions into thin wedges. Wash and clean the carrot (peel if necessary), then cut into thin slices. Wash, clean, and finely dice the zucchini. Wash the asparagus and chop off a generous portion of the stringy ends, then cut the stalks diagonally into slices as thick as a pinky finger. Wash the scallions, then remove the dark-green ends and the roots. Cut the scallions into thin rings. Wash the chili, remove the stem, and finely cut.

Wash the lemon in hot water and finely grate the zest. Squeeze out the juice. Boil 350 ml/12 fl oz water and pour over the couscous in a bowl, add the lemon juice and zest, salt, stir, and let soak for about 10 minutes.

Heat the olive oil in a large skillet. Sauté the onions in it over medium heat until they take on a bit of color, then add the pine nuts and the rest of the vegetables and cook until firm to the bite in 8–10 minutes. Be sure to stir regularly. Season to taste with salt, pepper, sugar, curry powder, and cayenne pepper (optional).

Fluff up the couscous with a fork, add to the vegetables in the skillet, and mix everything. Season once more to taste and drizzle some olive oil over it. Serve warm or cold with yogurt or sour cream.

OVEN PANCAKES WITH APPLES

When the sun peeks through the kitchen window and I feel like having a very special breakfast, then it has to be this recipe! You actually always have the ingredients at home, and yet: What comes out of the oven exudes more than just an incredible aroma. Puffed up to be airy light, resembling a soufflé, it ennobles every breakfast table. Allowed: Standing in front of the oven door and spying through the window to see how the pancake spreads out over the sides of the pan. Not allowed: Opening the oven door to get a closer look!

MAKES 4 PANCAKES (EACH 20 CM/ 8 INCH Ø)
PREPARATION TIME: 5 MINUTES PLUS PER PANCAKE 25 MINUTES BAKING TIME

250 ml/8.5 fl oz milk
150 g/5.25 oz flour
1 pinch of salt
2 tbsp sugar
1/4 tsp cinnamon powder
4 large eggs
2 small apples
4 tsp butter

To serve

Powdered sugar for dusting
Little flakes of butter to put on top
Maple syrup for drizzling

Preheat the oven to 200°C/390°F (convection oven 180°C/355°F). For the pancake batter, mix milk, flour, salt, sugar, cinnamon, and eggs by hand or with the whisk of the hand-held mixer until smooth. The batter shouldn't have any lumps in it, but also be sure not to beat it any longer than absolutely necessary.

Halve one apple, then peel one half of it and core. Cut it into wedges and little slices. (Always just cut the amount of apple that you need right away for one pancake because otherwise the apple slices will turn an unsightly brown.)

Heat 1 tsp butter in a small pan (20 cm/8 inch Ø; a heavy, cast-iron pan is best) and add the apple slices. Pour one-fourth of the batter into the pan so that it's as high as a finger is thick and spread until smooth. Put in the oven (middle) and bake the pancake until golden brown in about 20 minutes. It puffs up wonderfully and then should be served immediately because, like a soufflé, it will also collapse quickly.

Enjoy with powdered sugar, little butter flakes, and maple syrup. Use the same process with the rest of the batter and bake more pancakes.

CEVICHE WITH MANGO

Ceviche (pronounced: seh-vee-chay) is something like a national dish on the South and Central American continent. In countless variations and with regional characteristics, very fresh, raw fish for it is "cooked" in citrus juices. The resulting »Leche de Tigre« (tiger's milk) marinade is not only believed to have an aphrodisiac effect—it supposedly also works wonders for hangovers.

For me, this ceviche recipe—which contains an unbelievable amount of my favorite aromas—is simply the tastiest way to enjoy cold fish.

SERVES 4
PREPARATION TIME: 30 MINUTES
PLUS 2 HOURS MARINATING TIME

Ceviche

8 whole fresh, de-shelled scallops
200 g/7 oz very fresh whitefish fillet (such as cod or gilthead)
1 piece fresh ginger (about 1 cm/0.5 inch)
1/2–1 large red chili pepper
4 limes (of which 2 should be organic limes)
1 mango
1 avocado
1 scallion
1/4 bunch of cilantro
Sea salt
Freshly ground black pepper
2–3 tbsp olive oil

Bread Chips

150 g/5.25 oz baguette (from previous day)
1 squirt olive oil

Wash the scallops and the fillet, then dab dry with paper towels. Halve scallops horizontally and cut into 1-cm/0.5-inch cubes. Peel and finely grate the ginger and place in a bowl with the scallops. Wash the chili pepper, remove the stem, and finely chop. Remove any possibly existing bones in the fish fillets, then also cut into 1 cm/0.5 inch cubes and put in a different bowl together with the chili pepper. Wash the organic limes in hot water and finely grate the zest. Squeeze out all of the limes. Distribute the juice and zest between the two bowls. Stir briefly, cover, and let marinate in the refrigerator for about 2 hours.

Then stand the mango upright on a cutting board and cut off as much as you can to the left and right of the seed. Score the pulp down to the skin into a crosshatch pattern, but don't cut through the skin. Now you can invert the mango halves and easily cut the individual cubes from the skin. Also cut off the rest of the mango pulp from the seed and dice. Halve the avocado, remove the pit and dice finely. Peel the scallion and cut into fine rings. Combine everything in one bowl. Wash the cilantro, shake dry, finely chop (should be about 2 tbsp), and add to mixture.

Take the fish and scallops out of the refrigerator, place in a sieve, and let drain but save the marinade. Add fish and scallops to the prepared fruit and season the Ceviche to taste with salt, pepper, oil, and some of the marinade.

Goes well with bread chips: Cut the baguette into very thin slices. Heat the olive oil in a pan and toast the bread slices in it over medium to high heat on both sides until crisp.

GOOD-MORNING MUFFINS

These muffins are a typical example of how my own recipes are created. I had envisioned a juicy, fruity muffin that would be perfect with a glass of cold milk or juice for a quick breakfast. I began with a combination of dates and bananas and tried yogurt as the main ingredient, together with chopped dried fruit. After coming up with rather average baking results for the first three or four attempts, I replaced the dates with apples and the bananas with carrots. The yogurt also fell by the wayside at some point. But the addition of toasted hazelnuts was what made my new combination just perfect. My friend Kristin's opinion about them was to the point: "That's how muffins should taste!"

MAKES 12 MUFFINS
PREPARATION TIME: 20 MINUTES
PLUS 30–35 MINUTES BAKING TIME

80 g/3 oz ground hazelnuts
2–3 tbsp whole shelled hazelnuts
175 g/6.25 oz flour
2 tsp baking powder
1 pinch of salt
1 pinch of cinnamon powder
200 g/7 oz carrots
1 small apple
2 large eggs
150 g/5.25 oz raw cane sugar
100 g/3.5 oz sunflower oil

Plus

Muffin form for 12 muffins
12 muffin paper cups

Preheat the oven to 180°C/355°F (convection oven 160°C/320°F). Toast ground hazelnuts over medium heat in a dry pan until they slightly take on color and become fragrant, then let them cool off. Finely chop the shelled hazelnuts or put in a freezer bag and hit it a few times with a heavy pan. Mix flour, baking powder, salt, and cinnamon in a bowl. Wash the carrots (peel, if necessary) and finely grate. Quarter, core, peel, and cut the apple into fine slices.

Beat the eggs, cane sugar, and oil with the whisk of the hand-held mixer until frothy (2–3 minutes). Then mix in the ground hazelnuts, grated carrots (including any resulting juice), and the apple. Add the flour last. Continue to stir only until all of the ingredients are evenly mixed.

Line the muffin form with the paper cups. With the help of two tablespoons, fill with batter to just below the edge. Sprinkle the coarse pieces of hazelnut on top. Bake in the oven on the middle rack for 30–35 minutes until the muffins have risen nicely and taken on a bit of color. Insert a chopstick into the center: When the batter no longer sticks to it, the muffins are done. Take out of the oven, let cool for several minutes, and then remove from the form. Eat warm or cold—they will still be very moist the next day.

RED CABBAGE SALAD WITH FETA

Apart from the traditional side dish for the annual Christmas goose, red cabbage was neglected for quite a long time in my kitchen—despite the fact that this colorful head of cabbage is so versatile and healthy. It is astonishingly suitable for every type of crunchy raw-vegetable dish. But it is important to let it marinate for an adequate amount of time because that makes it more easily digestible. Combined with fruit and feta, red cabbage makes a colorful salad that is great to take along—whether to one of our traditional picnics on the Isar River or as a snack for a long day in front of the computer.

SERVES 4
PREPARATION TIME: 20 MINUTES
PLUS 1 HOUR OF MARINATING

- 1 small head of red cabbage (about 300 g/10.5 oz)
- 1 fennel bulb (with the fronds)
- 1 slightly tart apple
- 3 oranges (of which 1 should be organic)
- 3 tbsp white wine vinegar
- 1 pinch of sea salt
- 1 tsp sugar
- Freshly ground white pepper
- 100 ml/3.5 fl oz canola oil
- 100 g/3.5 oz sheep cheese

Remove the outer leaves of the red cabbage. Slice the cabbage into quarters and remove the core from each piece. Either finely cut or grate the cabbage quarters. Wash the fennel. Cut off the fronds and set aside for later use. Then cut the bulb into quarters and also finely slice or grate. Quarter, core, peel, and grate the apple. Mix all of these salad ingredients in a bowl.

For the dressing, wash the organic orange in hot water and finely grate the zest. Then cut the fruit in half and squeeze out the juice. Thoroughly stir the zest and juice together with vinegar, salt, sugar, pepper, and canola oil. Pour the dressing over the prepared salad, cover, and let marinate in the refrigerator for about 1 hour. Mix it thoroughly every 30 minutes.

Then cut off all of the peel from the remaining two oranges with a sharp knife so that the white skin is also removed. Now cut out the individual fruit segments between the segment walls, save any juice that comes out and pour everything on the salad. Finely chop the fennel fronds. To serve the marinated salad, crumble the sheep cheese over it and garnish with orange fillets and fennel fronds.

RICE PUDDING CUPS WITH FRUIT

Maybe the principle is similar to the baby scheme; in any case, I have a weakness for everything that comes served in pretty little serving jars. The result is that our kitchen cabinets now have an alarming selection of old yogurt jars—in which I like to serve desserts or homemade fruit yogurts—piled up in them. This recipe for an especially creamy rice pudding not only peps up a brunch but also keeps in the refrigerator for a few days as a sweet snack—for which the individual small jars are obviously the best!

MAKES 8–10 LITTLE GLASS JARS (OF ABOUT 120 G/4.25 OZ EACH)
PREPARATION TIME: 30 MINUTES FOR THE RICE
PLUS 10–15 MINUTES PER TOPPING

Rice Pudding

1 vanilla bean
1 l/1 US quart milk (possibly a bit more)
50 g/1.75 oz sugar
1 pinch of salt
200 g/7 oz rice pudding
100 g/3.5 oz cream

plus

Strawberry Topping

200 g/7 oz strawberries
2–3 tbsp vanilla sugar
1 tbsp lemon juice

or

Caramel-Apple Topping

2 apples
75 g/2.75 oz sugar
150 g/5.25 oz cream
1/4 tsp cinnamon powder

Rice Pudding

Slice the vanilla pod lengthwise and scrape out the pulp. Boil the milk with the vanilla pulp and pod, sugar, and salt in a large pot. Stir in the rice and cook over low heat (don't forget to stir continuously so that nothing sticks to the bottom). If the pudding becomes too firm, add a bit more milk to it.

As soon as the rice is soft (do the first "bite test" already after 20 minutes), remove the vanilla pod, and stir in the cream. The rice should now have a soft-flowing consistency so that it stays creamy even when cold. Let cool.

Toppings

Either wash the strawberries, dab dry, remove the stems, and cut into small pieces. Then mix with the vanilla sugar and lemon juice and macerate for 5 minutes.

Or quarter, core, and peel the apples and then dice finely. Let the sugar caramelize to a golden-yellow in a large pan without stirring over medium heat. Add cream while stirring (don't be startled if it briefly foams up) and stir the caramel until smooth. Season with cinnamon, add the apples, and let simmer for 3–5 minutes over a low heat.

Finish

Either first fill the little jars with the rice pudding and then divide the macerated strawberries among them. Or put the caramel apple in the little jars and top with the rice.

Tip: A jam funnel makes it easier to fill narrow little jars and prevents spills.

FRIENDSHIP
goes through the stomach

FRIENDSHIP GOES THROUGH THE STOMACH

What do you do when you are thousands of miles away from your family, and maybe even live and work on another continent? You need good friends who stick by you through thick and thin, share your interests, and are almost like a substitute family for you. Our American friend Craig must have had thoughts like this when he—long before we met him—started a regular movie night in Vienna with a few colleagues from work.

When he and his girlfriend Dagi ended up in Munich because of a job change, it certainly didn't distract them from their passion for films. They also found a movie theater here that had English sneak previews on its program and the new colleagues from work quickly responded with enthusiasm to the idea of a movie night.

The Friday evening became a fixed date as a growing number of movie fans met to have dinner and let themselves be surprised afterward by a (hopefully) great film.

This lovely tradition has already been going on for years and we—sometimes in a larger, sometimes in a smaller group—still collectively ring in the weekend, chat about the events of the past week, or make plans for outings. This usually happens at our favorite bar, which not only has the very best burgers in the city on its menu but giant leather sofas and a relaxed atmosphere that is just perfect for putting a stressful work week behind you in pleasant company.

The film fans have turned into real friends through time, which is no wonder because we all share the same passion for eating, cooking, and partying with each other. Lucky for me—there are always enough volunteers whenever I need guinea pigs to sample the umpteenth version of my butter caramels that I bring with me.

Since the films are shown in their original version, it's also a good opportunity to invite foreign colleagues or friends and make it easier for them to get a good start in Munich through these first contacts.

On the other hand, the fact that we all come from different countries and cultural backgrounds is also wonderfully enriching for us:

Sylvie—our French wine expert—accepts our requests for souvenirs of a culinary nature before she goes home on visits, Ruth showed me how labor-intensive it is for her Ethiopian family to make samosas, and Carlos knows the latest secrets about Spanish gazpacho and more.

When Thanksgiving weekend is just around the corner in the USA, our American ex-pats here make sure we have an unforgettable Thanksgiving dinner, to which everyone makes a contribution—despite the little obstacles: Where do you get the pecans or fresh cranberries and yams, how do you carve a pumpkin without hurting yourself, and what should you do when the oven is simply too small for the turkey?

We were really fortunate the last time when the Bavarian butcher's shop on the corner declared that it was willing to roast it for us. All of the guests were obviously very amused to see that the gigantic thermobox used to transport the bird was kept warm under a pile of duvets - of all things! And while happily digging into the abundant Thanksgiving buffet and exchanging our experiences and recipes, we already collected ideas for the next mutual trip back to our favorite alpine pasture—because of the food.

Hausgemachte
Entensülze mit
frischen Pfifferlingen,
dazu Röstkartoffeln
€12,90

YAHOO!

DAGI'S MUESLI
BIRCHER STYLE

Our friends Dagi and Craig are known for their unconventional ideas, which is why no one was surprised when they invited us to a brunch with the motto of "Bob Ross." Even today, people can still learn how to paint happy little bushes from the painter with the gentle voice and his trademark Afro hairdo on nighttime television. So the brunch included a separate studio room where everyone could watch his videos and try out Ross's techniques on a canvas on their own. That was a lot of fun for young and old!

Although I don't believe that we discovered any genuine talent that morning, the brunch buffet offered something for every taste—from Bavarian veal sausage with pretzels to mini-pizzas to blueberry waffles. But the hit was Dagi's muesli, which she made according to one of her mother's recipes: Even its pink color was a real eye-catcher, not to even mention the taste. I still have a suspicion that I polished off almost the entire bowl on my own...

INGREDIENTS

For 4: 250 ml/8.5 fl oz milk (or water) | 100 g/3.5 oz baby rolled oats | 75 g/2.75 oz dried fruit (such as dates and/or figs) | 100 g/3.5 oz shelled hazelnuts | 1 fully ripe banana | 100 g/3.5 oz raspberries (frozen or fresh) | 300 g/10.5 oz Greek full-fat yoghurt or natural yoghurt | small cut pieces of fruit (such as plums, bananas, or apples) for garnish

PREPARATION

This muesli leaves you enough leeway to change it according to your own taste, gives you a healthy start to your day and is only sweetened with fruit. Does it get any better than that?

THE BASE

Heat the milk, pour over the oats, and let soak for at least 1 hour.

THE SWEETNESS

Soak the dried fruit in 75 ml/2.5 fl oz of water for 1 hour, then mix into a smooth paste using an electric grinder or with the hand-held blender. The fruit puree provides natural sweetness—add tablespoons of it to the oats until it's sweet enough for you. You can keep the rest in the refrigerator (in a canning jar, for example) for several days.

THE NUTS

Toast the hazelnuts in a dry pan until they are fragrant, then chop coarsely. Mix two-thirds of them into the muesli and keep the rest as garnish.

THE FRUIT

Peel the banana, mash with a fork, and mix into the muesli. Stir in defrosted (with juice) or fresh raspberries that are slightly mashed.

THE FINISH

Stir in the 200 g/7 oz yogurt and put the muesli into small bowls. Crown each of them with a dollop of the remaining yogurt, the fruit for garnishing and the rest of the chopped nuts.

TORTILLA DE BETANZOS

When Anja and Carlos invite us to one of their legendary Spanish evenings, we always know that there will be a real feast waiting for us. The action is usually also concentrated in the kitchen here—just like any good party. While the hostess chops mountains of potatoes for the tortillas together with her boyfriend Juan, I always try to coax one secret or another from the Galician kitchen out of them. And this also worked for this tortilla, which has a wonderfully moist and liquid inside.

INGREDIENTS

For 1 tortilla (20–22 cm/8–8.75 inch Ø): 500 g/ 1.1 lb potatoes (best between waxy and mealy) | 1 garlic clove | 1 onion | 75 g/2.75 oz chorizo (cured spiced pork sausage) | 4–5 very fresh large eggs | sea salt | freshly ground white pepper | about 300 ml/10 fl oz olive oil

PREPARATION

Peel, wash, and cut the potatoes into cubes of equal size (about 1 cm/0.5 inch). Peel and mince the garlic, peel and cut the onion into coarse chunks, and peel and finely dice the chorizo. Beat the eggs in a large bowl with the whisk and season with salt and pepper until spicy.

Heat plenty of olive oil in a large pan. Add the potatoes and deep-fry over high heat until they are well-done and golden brown (or even darker, if you like them that way), which takes about 10 minutes. The potatoes should just be covered by the oil. If necessary, simply deep-fry them in two batches. Remove with the slotted spoon and let drain on two paper towels. Now deep-fry the onions in the same way. When they have just taken on a bit of color, also add the garlic for a maximum of 1 minute. Then put everything in a colander and save the oil that drips off. Use the remaining oil in the pan to sauté the chorizo briefly.

Mix the potatoes, onions, garlic, and chorizo into the eggs. Heat 2 tbsp of the reserved oil in a small pan (20–22 cm/8–8.75 inch Ø). Pour the potato mixture into the pan and cook for 2–3 minutes over medium to high heat. To make sure that the tortilla doesn't stick to the pan, run along the edge with a wood spatula and carefully shake the pan (you might even want to peek under the tortilla to make sure that it doesn't become too dark.)

Put a large, flat plate face down on the pan, bravely flip the tortilla onto it (otherwise you'll have a terrible mess!), and—now the other way around—let it slide back into the pan. Very briefly cook on the second side (for a maximum of 1 minute), which keeps the tortilla liquid in the center and lets it taste really juicy. On the other hand, if you would prefer to enjoy a well-done tortilla, cook it for 3–4 minutes on each side over medium heat.

kneaded & baked

ORANGE BRIOCHE

My grandmother Luise loved to bake with fresh yeast. I watched her and helped with the sweet yeast dumplings and damson cake for years, which is why I am very familiar with the entire process. If you pay attention to a few basic rules, making yeast dough is as easy as pie: Only work with really fresh yeast, avoid any direct contact between the butter and the yeast, and be sure to let the dough rise in a draft-free and warm place while covered. If necessary, this place can also be your own oven: Simply preheat for 1–2 minutes to 100°C/210°F and then turn it off immediately—this is how the yeast dough gets a cozy warm spot and can rise wonderfully.

MAKES 12 PIECES
PREPARATION TIME: 20 MINUTES
PLUS 1–1/2 HOURS FOR RISING AND
20 MINUTES FOR BAKING

- 20 g/0.75 oz fresh yeast
- 1 large egg
- 250 ml/8.5 fl oz milk
- 75 g/2.75 oz butter (plus a little more for the muffin pan and the shiny finish)
- 500 g/1.1 lb oz flour
- 75 g/2.75 oz sugar
- 1 organic orange
- 1 pinch of salt

Plus

12-cup muffin pan

All ingredients should be at room temperature, so take the yeast and egg out of the refrigerator ahead of time. Heat the milk in a saucepan until lukewarm, and melt the butter in a second pan.

Sift flour into a large bowl and make a well in the center. Crumble the yeast into it, add 1 pinch of sugar and pour in enough milk to cover the yeast. Cover the bowl with a dish towel and let the sponge rise in a warm place for about 15 minutes until it forms bubbles.

Wash the orange with hot water and finely grate the zest. Put in a bowl with the remaining milk, the rest of the sugar, egg, and salt. Knead everything into a smooth dough. You can either do this with your hands or the kneading hooks of the hand-held mixer (also great: the food processor). The dough is ready when it can easily be lifted from the sides of the bowl (add flour by the tablespoon if it still feels too sticky). Cover and let rise again in a warm place, until the dough has almost doubled its volume. This should take about one hour.

Preheat the oven to 200°C/390°F (convection oven 180°C/355°F). Grease the cups of the muffin pan with butter. Knead the dough one last time and divide into 12 equally large pieces. Then form each of these pieces into 3 balls of equal size, and place them in the middle of a cup. Brush with a little melted butter, cover with foil, and let rise one last time for about 15–20 minutes. Then place in the oven (second lowest rack) and bake for about 20 minutes until golden brown. Remove from oven and let cool briefly before taking out of the form. For extra shine, brush the brioche once more with a little butter.

Sunshine-yellow saffron brioche: For yeast bread with a captivating saffron aroma, simply grind 1/4 – 1/2 tsp of saffron threads in the mortar with 1 tbsp sugar and add this to the milk before warming it. It replaces the orange zest.

BANANA-COCONUT CAKE

I was more than happy to adopt a ritual that I grew up with—baking at least one cake every weekend. Depending on the season, this may be a fresh fruit cake with strawberries or apples—or, as in this recipe, it may also be a moist cake from a simple sponge mixture. In this case, the coconut flakes and bananas ensure that the cake still tastes nice and juicy even after a few days.

Incidentally, it doesn't matter if the bananas you use have seen better days. That's what makes this one of my standard recipes when a few bananas in the fruit basket are already overripe...

MAKES 1 SPRING FORM (26 CM/10 INCH Ø) OR A RECTANGULAR 30 CM/12 INCH LONG CAKE PAN
PREPARATION TIME: 15 MINUTES PLUS 45–50 MINUTES BAKING TIME

- 150 g/5.25 oz room-temperature butter (plus a little more for the form)
- 250 g/9 oz flour (plus a little more for the form)
- 125 ml/4.25 fl oz milk
- 1 tsp baking soda
- 100 g/3.5 oz raw cane (Demerara) sugar
- 3 large eggs
- 3–4 very ripe bananas (about 300 g/10.5 oz)
- 100 g/3.5 oz coconut flakes
- 3 tsp baking powder

Preheat the oven to 180°C/355°F (convection oven 160°/320°F). Grease and flour the spring form or rectangular cake pan or line with baking paper. Pour the milk into a small bowl and dissolve the baking soda in it.

Place butter, sugar, and eggs into a large bowl and beat until foamy with the whisk of the hand mixer. Peel the bananas, mash with a fork and mix in briefly with the coconut flakes. Sift the flour and baking powder over the foamy mixture, pour in the milk, and mix everything by hand with a large wooden spoon. The batter should fall heavily from the spoon.

Fill the batter into the prepared form and bake in the oven on the second lowest rack for 45–50 minutes. Pierce with a skewer: When the skewer comes out clean, the cake is done. Otherwise, bake for a few more minutes. Take the cake out of the oven, let cool for 10 minutes, and then remove from the form.

GRISSINI

When I spent my school vacations with my grandparents in Italy, there were always two highlights for me when we went to a restaurant: Firstly, the legendary desserts. And secondly, the dust-dry grissini, which were sealed into plastic wrap and part of the coperto, the place setting that was purchased separately. The latter have very little in common with home-made grissini sticks. Grissini are quick to make and are the perfect addition to an Italian meal with friends or for a lazy evening on the sofa.

MAKES 25–30 PIECES
PREPARATION TIME: 20 MINUTES
PLUS 20 MINUTES FOR RISING AND
15 MINUTES BAKING TIME

10 g/0.35 oz fresh yeast (1 tsp of dry yeast can also be used as a substitute)
250 g/9 oz bread flour
Heaping 1/2 tsp of fine sea salt
1 tbsp olive oil

Sprinkle with
Coarse sea salt
Freshly grated Parmesan
Dukkah (see page 168)

Stir the yeast into 125 ml/4.25 fl oz lukewarm water. Mix the flour with the salt in a bowl and add the olive oil and yeast water to it. Knead everything by hand or with the kneading hooks of the hand mixer until the dough is nice and smooth (at least 5 minutes). Shape into a ball, cover with the dish towel, and let rise for 20 minutes in a warm place.

Preheat the oven to 200°C/390°F (convection oven 180°C/355°F) and cover a baking sheet with baking paper. Roll the dough out in the shape of a rectangle until it is about 1/2 cm/1/4 inch thick. Cut into small, finger-thick strips with a sharp knife. Use both hands to roll these into thick ropes. Then, for...

Grissini Natural, place the dough ropes on the baking sheet, brush with a small amount of water and sprinkle with a little coarse sea salt.

Grissini with Parmesan, brush the dough ropes with a small amount of water, sprinkle with freshly grated Parmesan and roll on the work surface again until it is completely covered in cheese. Then place on the sheet.

Grissini with Dukkah (my favorites), brush the dough ropes with a small amount of water, sprinkle with the dukkah, and roll on the surface again until they are all evenly coated with the mixture of spices. Then place on the sheet.

Bake for about 15 minutes in the middle of the oven so that the tips take on some color. The grissini should stay relatively light otherwise (exception: Parmesan). Take out of the oven and let cool on a wire rack, then serve with an aperitif or appetizer. If you store them in an airtight container, the grissini will stay crisp for a few days.

KIRWA CAKE

At home, we have many names for this moist sheet cake but the most popular are probably kirwa cake (the colloquial version of Kirchweih—annual church festival—cake) and cheesecake. This cake is typical of the Upper Palatinate region where I grew up and can be found at every family celebration and village festival. Unfortunately, my Grandma Luise took her original recipe to the grave with her—so I needed a number of attempts before my family could confirm that my cake "tastes like the one Grandma made". No matter whether it's still slightly warm from the oven or eaten cold the next day, everyone loves this cake.

MAKES 1 BAKING SHEET
(ABOUT 42 X 38 CM/17 X 15 INCHES)
PREPARATION TIME: 20 MINUTES
PLUS 1–1 1/4 HOURS RISING TIME AND
20–25 MINUTES FOR BAKING.

Yeast Batter

375 g/13.25 oz flour (possibly a bit more)
20 g/0.75 oz fresh yeast
50 g/1.75 oz sugar
125 ml/4.25 fl oz lukewarm milk
50 g/1.75 oz soft butter
1 room-temperature medium egg
1 pinch salt

Semolina Topping

1/4–1/2 tsp saffron threads (possibly a bit more)
150 g/5.25 oz sugar
750 ml/25.5 fl oz milk
150 g/5.25 oz semolina
125 g/4.5 oz butter
1 medium egg
Raisins (optional)

For the batter, put flour in a bowl and make a well in the middle. Crumble yeast into the well, sprinkle a pinch of sugar over it, and pour enough lukewarm milk over it to cover the yeast evenly. Briefly stir the yeast milk, then cover the bowl with a dish towel and let the sponge rise in a warm place for 15 minutes until the first bubbles become visible.

Add the rest of the milk, the remaining sugar, butter, egg, and salt. Knead the mixture with the kneading hooks of the hand mixer until the batter can easily be lifted from the side of the bowl. If the batter is still very sticky, add flour by the tablespoon. Lightly dust with flour, cover, and let rise in a warm place for about 1 hour (if you need to finish more quickly, then 30 minutes will also suffice).

Preheat over to 180°C/355°F (convection oven 160°C/320°F) and line a baking sheet with baking paper. Briefly knead the dough once more, roll out on the floured work surface until it is approximately the size of the sheet and about 0.5 cm/0.25 inch thick. Then spread out on the sheet and pull into shape. Keep covered until you work with it again.

For the topping, finely grind the saffron with 1 tsp sugar in the mortar. Boil the milk and stir in the semolina, saffron, rest of the sugar, butter, and the egg until it becomes an even paste. The topping should now have turned a brilliant yellow color. If not, add a little saffron. Remove from the stove. Then immediately spread onto the batter. If you like, you can sprinkle it with raisins. Bake in the oven (middle rack) for 20–25 minutes, but make sure that the bottom doesn't get too dark. Let cool and cut into square pieces.

QUICK FLAT BREAD WITH DUKKAH

Dukkah is a spice mixture with nuts, which I sampled for the first time at a little spice bazaar in Egypt—but I only really learned to appreciate it much later. With the homemade flat bread from the pan (this can be prepared much more quickly than you might imagine!) and a fruity olive oil, it is well-suited as an appetizer for an oriental meal. Just tear the flat bread into small pieces, dunk it first in the olive oil, and then in the dukkah.

MAKES 8–10 PIECES
PREPARATION TIME: 1–1 1/4 HOURS

Yeast Dough

- 20 g/0.75 oz fresh yeast (use 1 level tsp of dry yeast as a substitute)
- 1/4 tsp cumin seeds (optional)
- 300 g/10.5 oz bread flour (plus a little extra for rolling)
- Heaping 1/2 tsp fine sea salt
- 1 tbsp olive oil

Dukkah

- 3 tbsp hazelnuts
- 2 tbsp pine nuts
- 2 tbsp sesame seeds
- 2 tbsp coriander seeds
- 2 tbsp cumin seeds
- 1 tbsp black peppercorns
- 1 tsp Fleur de Sel/Maldon sea salt

Plus

Olive oil for the pan and for dipping

For the dough, combine yeast and 200 ml/7 fl oz lukewarm water in a bowl. Finely grind the cumin in the mortar, then mix together with the flour and salt in a large bowl.

Add the dissolved yeast and the oil, then knead everything into a smooth dough with the kneading hooks of the hand mixer. Dust with flour, cover, and let rise for 15–30 minutes.

In the meantime, prepare the dukkah: Chop the hazelnuts and pine nuts in the food chopper, but not too finely. Then place in a dry pan with the sesame and toast over medium heat until golden brown. Remove from the pan and let cool. Also toast the spices (except for the salt) in a dry pan for a few minutes over medium heat, and then finely grind in the mortar. Mix the nuts, spices, and salt and store in a dark, airtight container.

Preheat the oven to 80°C/175°F (convection oven 60°C/140°F). Briefly knead the dough once more, and then divide into pieces that are more or less the same size. It should yield 8–10. Roll out one piece of dough on the floured work surface with a rolling pin into flat bread that is very thin and as round as possible. At the same time, heat a large pan (over medium to high heat), add some olive oil, and place the first flat bread in the pan. Sprinkle with a little olive oil. As soon as the bottom shows its first darker spots (which happens very quickly!), turn over the flat bread and finish baking. Place in the oven and keep warm. Prepare the rest of the flat bread from the remaining dough, one piece at a time.

Place the flat bread, olive oil, and dukkah on the table so that everyone can help themselves to it.

1-2-3-POPPY-SEED CAKE

If you like Austrian sweet dishes and poppy seed, then you'll love this cake. Not just because it's unbelievably moist, but also because it's undoubtedly the quickest and least complicated cake to whip up in my entire repertoire.

In order for the poppy seeds to develop their full aroma, they should be used as freshly ground as possible (they will become rancid otherwise). The "grinding" is actually a "crushing"—as my spice dealer recently explained to me. If you are like me and don't have your own poppy-seed mill or crusher, it's best to have the grinding done by the poppy-seed dealer of your choice. A labor-intensive compromise is the mortar.

FOR 1 RECTANGULAR CAKE PAN (30 CM/12 INCHES IN LENGTH) OR WHICHEVER CAKE FORM YOU PREFER
PREPARATION TIME: 10 MINUTES PLUS 45–50 MINUTES FOR BAKING

- 250 g/9 oz soft butter (plus a bit more for the pan)
- 5 room-temperature medium or large eggs
- 75 g/2.75 oz room-temperature crème fraîche
- 200 g/7 oz sugar
- 1 organic lemon
- 100 g/3.5 oz freshly ground poppy seeds
- 200 g/7 oz flour (plus a bit more for the pan)
- 2 tbsp baking powder
- Icing sugar for dusting

All of the ingredients should be at room temperature for optimal baking results, so be sure to take the butter, eggs, and crème fraîche out of the refrigerator ahead of time. Preheat the oven to 180°C/355°F (convection oven 160°C/320°F). Brush the selected baking pan with butter and dust evenly with flour.

Beat the butter and sugar until creamy with the whisk of the hand mixer (or with a food processor). Then gradually add the eggs while mixing continuously. Wash the lemon with hot water and grate the zest on a fine grater directly into the bowl. Add the crème fraîche and poppy seeds and mix in as well. Put the flour in the bowl, sprinkle the baking powder over it, and mix everything well one last time.

Fill the batter into the pan and bake in the oven on the second lowest rack (or just below the middle) for 45–50 minutes. Pierce the cake with a skewer. When the skewer comes out clean, the cake is done. Otherwise, bake for a few more minutes. Take the cake out of the oven and let cool for 10 minutes, then turn over the pan onto a plate to remove it. When the cake has cooled completely, dust it with icing sugar.

LIME-MATCHA COOKIES

New trends spread on food blogs at a breathtaking speed. A good example of this is Kelli Bernard's Green Tea Sweets. In her blog, which
was originally dedicated to all sweet temptations (www.lovescool.com), Kelli has documented her path from an IT career to her own teahouse in New York (Amai) and set off a landslide of enthusiasm with this recipe. Food-bloggers in Italy, Estonia, Australia, Singapore, Mauritius, and many other places were so turned on by her matcha cookies that they received one hymn of praise after the other.

My variation of Kelli's recipe has a hint of fresh lime that harmonizes wonderfully with green tea. The cookies literally melt on your tongue and are wonderful with tea!

MAKES 2 COOKIE SHEETS
PREPARATION TIME: 10 MINUTES PLUS 1 HOUR FOR COOLING AND 10–15 MINUTES FOR BAKING

- 80 g/3 oz icing sugar
- 2 tsp matcha tea (powder made of green tea leaves, available in tea shops)
- 3 organic limes
- 150 g/5.25 oz cold butter
- 1 pinch of salt
- 200 g/7 oz flour (plus a bit more for rolling out the dough)
- 25–50 g/1–1.75 oz cornstarch
- 3 medium egg yolks
- 75 g/2.75 oz sugar

It's best to sift the icing sugar into the bowl of a food processor and mix with the tea powder. Wash 1 lime with hot water and finely grate the zest. Cut the butter into small cubes and add to the powdered sugar together with the lime zest and salt. Mix with the flat blade until it becomes a bright green, smooth mixture (if necessary, you can use the hand mixer with kneading hooks instead of the food processor). Then mix in the flour and cornstarch at the end.

Divide the dough into two pieces and shape each into a finger-thick slab. Wrap in foil. The dough must rest for at least 1 hour in the refrigerator so that it becomes firm. But I often let it cool for a longer time (even up to 2 days is not a problem) so it doesn't get soft so quickly when working with it.

Preheat the oven to 170°C/340°F (convection oven 150°C/300°F) and line a baking sheet with baking paper. Wash the remaining limes with hot water, finely grate the zest, and grind as finely as possible in the mortar with 1 tbsp of sugar. Mix with the rest of the sugar and place in a bowl.

Dust a work surface with a bit of flour and roll out the dough—the original Green Tea Sweets are rather thick at more than 1 cm/0.5 inch, but I prefer my cookies thinner (just 0.5 cm/0.25 inch). Cut cookies out of the dough. The simpler and more compact the cookie cutters are, the easier it is to handle the dough (if necessary, put in the refrigerator and let it become firm again). Carefully roll the cookies in the lime sugar—completely or just the edges. Place on the sheet and bake in the oven (middle rack) according to their thickness and shape for 10–15 minutes. They are perfect when they are baked all the way through but haven't turned a golden color yet. Take them out and let them cool off.

Tip: Kelli recommends storing the cookies in opaque jars because they keep their intensive green color longer that way.

ONION BREAD WITH MALT BEER

My love of malt beer started in my childhood: If the children wanted to have a beverage with a foamy crown like the beer that the adults drank, the younger generation got alcohol-free malt beer—it was quite sweet and certainly not to everyone's taste. It's different in this bread: The malt beer gives it more than just the rustic, dark color. Its sweetness also harmonizes wonderfully with the sweet aroma of the roasted onions.

MAKES 1 BAGUETTE-SHAPED LOAF OF BREAD
PREPARATION TIME: 30 MINUTES PLUS ROUGHLY 8 HOURS FOR RISING AND 25–30 MINUTES FOR BAKING

- 300 g/10.5 oz bread flour (plus a bit more to work with)
- 1 level tsp fine sea salt
- 10 g/0.35 oz fresh yeast
- 200 ml/7 fl oz room-temperature malt beer
- 2 onions
- 1 tbsp butter

Plus

- Baking stone (you can use a normal baking sheet and line it with baking paper as a substitute)
- Coarse corn meal for dusting
- 1 handful of ice cubes

It's best to mix the flour and salt in the bowl of a food processor. Mix the yeast and malt beer, then add to the flour. Knead everything with the kneading hooks of the food processor into a relatively firm dough—it should still be slightly sticky. Otherwise, add more flour by the tablespoon (instead of the food processor, you can also use the hand mixer with kneading hooks). Cover the dough and let it rise in the refrigerator overnight or for at least 6 hours. (Super idea: Place the dough in a slightly oiled plastic jar that closes tightly to let it rise. This stops the top of the dough from drying out.)

The risen dough should be taken out of the refrigerator 1 hour before you continue working with it. In the meantime, peel the onions and cut into coarse cubes. Heat butter in a pan until foamy, then sauté the onions in it until golden brown over medium heat. Let cool.

Knead the cooled onions evenly into the dough and roll it into one long baguette on a lightly floured work surface. Dust with flour and let rise under a dish towel for another 30–45 minutes. During this time, preheat the oven with the baking stone (at the height of the lower third) for at least 30 minutes to full power (my regular oven easily reaches temperatures between 240–250°C/465–480°F with enough preheating time), but it should be at least 230°C/445°F. Also place an ovenproof form (such as a casserole dish) at the bottom of the oven.

Use a serrated knife to make several 1-cm/0.5-inch deep diagonal slashes in the bread. Dust a bread peel with coarse corn meal and carefully let the bread slide onto the baking stone on it (or use your hands as a substitute). Put ice cubes on the bottom of the form because they create steam during baking (which is good for the bread crust). Close the oven door as quickly as possible and spray water on the oven walls twice during the next 10 minutes, which also creates more steam. Bake the bread for 25–30 minutes until it has a nice golden-brown crust and the bottom of the bread sounds hollow when you knock on it. Take it out of the oven and let it cool completely on a wire rack. Tastes best either fresh or toasted.

CHOCOLATE MINIS

If you have ever tried a chocolate cake made (almost) without flour, you will never turn back. Compact and super-chocolaty, every bite melts on your tongue—it's actually almost more of a dessert than a cake. Since the batter is very rich, I like to use it for mini-muffins. They are ideal when you have a little craving for a chocolate snack (great for parties). The decorative icing of white chocolate and chopped pistachios make them extra special.

MAKES 20 PIECES
PREPARATION TIME: 30 MINUTES
PLUS 15 MINUTES FOR BAKING

Batter

200 g/7 oz high-quality dark chocolate (60–70 % cocoa)
200 g/7 oz butter (plus a bit more for the muffin tin)
250 g/9 oz sugar
4 large eggs
3 tbsp flour

Decoration

200 g/7 oz white chocolate
2 tbsp chopped pistachios

Plus

Baking pan for 20 mini-muffins

Preheat the oven to 190°C/375°F (convection oven 175°C/345°F). Brush the cups of the muffin pan with butter.

For the batter, break the chocolate into pieces and place into a larger metal bowl with the butter. Melt above a hot bain-marie. Mix in the sugar and set the bowl aside for a few minutes to cool. Then work in one egg after the other and stir each time until the egg has completely "melted" into the chocolate mixture. This will change the consistency of the mixture from fluid at the beginning to almost pudding-like at the end. Stir in the flour last.

Fill the batter into the tin cups and place the pan in the middle of the oven. Bake the minis for about 15 minutes. They should be stable enough to hold their form when you turn them over, but still have a soft core. If you aren't sure, you can nibble on a test muffin... When the muffins are done, take them out of the oven, let cool for 10 minutes and then turn the form upside down to remove them.

When the chocolate minis have cooled completely, break the white chocolate into pieces for the decoration. Place in a small metal bowl and melt above the bain-marie. Cover the minis with the chocolate and sprinkle with the pistachios.

Chocolate Cake: It's just as easy to bake a flat cake out of the batter. Line the bottom of a spring form (about 26 cm/10 inch Ø) with baking paper, grease the sides, and fill the batter into it. Bake in the oven (heat as above) for 22–25 minutes. The cake is done when the center is still minimally soft and feels like pudding. Serve while still warm with whipped cream, vanilla ice cream or sauce, and fresh fruit.

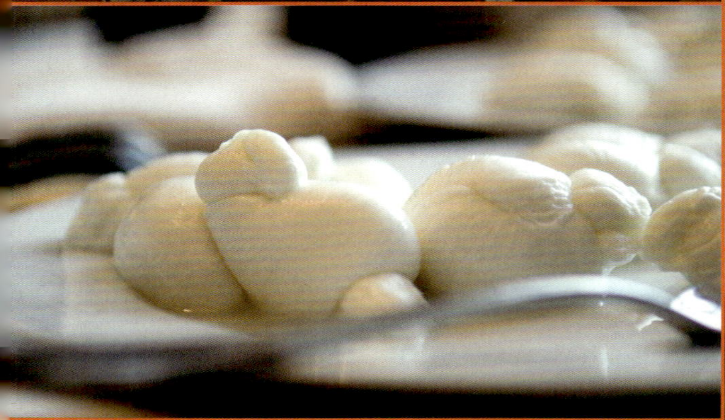

BELLA ITALIA

Where grannies throw ice-cream cones
and wooden clogs are banned.

BELLA ITALIA

Ever since the late 1950s, Italy was the declared favorite travel destination of my grandparents. Yellowed pictures in their old photo albums tell of camping vacations on the Italian lakes, sightseeing in Rome or beach vacations by the Adriatic Sea.

I also share their enthusiasm for the Italian way of life. From early childhood on, I always accompanied my grandparents when they headed for Italy.

With their old Ascona, which my grandfather had loaded to the roof with tons of luggage, we usually headed south on the highway about two or three hours after midnight. Although it was quite progressive in those days, my grandfather always let grandmother take the wheel because he thought she was the better driver.

While we slowly wound our way over the Plocken Pass, the first rays of sunshine got us in the mood for the vacation and Grandma Luise stopped at a service area to drink her first coffee on Italian soil. The last few hours passed very quickly. Even as we entered the driveway of Villa Mansutti, we were greeted loudly by the owner. Signora Mansutti was the epitome of an Italian landlady–short, wiry, with sun-weathered skin, and a penetrating laugh. Then there was a big hello with the other guests. Many of them were long-time friends of my grandparents and also spent their vacations at the sea every year, bringing along their own children or grandchildren.

These weeks couldn't have been more wonderful: Even though each family had its own apartment with a kitchen, the doors were usually left open and everyone often shopped and cooked together. My grandmother was in her element when they went to the market, where she haggled about the prices with the dealers while they tried to impress her with a few scraps of German ("no worm in cherry"). To the delight of us children, pasta was obviously on the menu more than usual. And sometimes we were allowed to sample something sweet at Signora Mansutti's place: If she was in a good mood, there was homemade cake. But if we had once again broken the top law of the house rules (no wooden clogs on the staircase!), she stood angrily in the door with fists pressed against her hips and scolded like crazy.

In the evenings, all of the families strolled through the town together before heading for a trattoria. If an international soccer tournament was in progress, the men crowded around the television while everyone else succumbed to the charm of the Italian open-air movie theater. In this case, the "movie theater" consisted of a few rows of rickety wooden chairs in the courtyard, usually with a limited program: Adriano Celentano, Bud Spencer, or an old Disney film. There was ice cream for everyone on the way home. However, not only did the Italian ice-cream parlors have a selection that we could only dream about in Germany; the owners also knew how to pile up huge portions masterfully on the cone with their scoops. We still puzzle today whether Grandma Luise was dissatisfied with her choice of ice cream or whether too much red wine was involved when she smacked her ice-cream cone in the middle of a parked car's windshield without any warning. We only noticed that the driver was still in the car when he jumped out of it, snorting with rage...

Through the years and with every new vacation destination, my picture of Italian cuisine has changed because of the major culinary differences between the individual regions. But this has only increased my love of the Italian kitchen.

If I had to name one single country whose people know how to celebrate the simplest dishes, who use "food" as a synonym for "lifestyle"–it could only be Bella Italia.

ASTA

TOMATO FOCACCIA

During our most recent visit to Italy, I discovered a new variation of breakfast for myself: Tomato foccacia that is still warm and smells wonderfully of rosemary, with fresh buffalo mozzarella. This is an unusual start into the day for someone with a sweet tooth like me. The focaccia is also just as good as bread to take to a barbecue (perfectly suited for dipping in good olive oil) and can be baked with all kinds of ingredients like olives, pesto, nuts, or anchovy fillets. Which is why it's by far the most frequently baked bread in my own kitchen.

INGREDIENTS

For 1 focaccia: 20 g/0.75 oz fresh yeast (but 1 tsp dry yeast works as well) | 250 g/9 oz bread flour | 1 level tsp fine sea salt | top-quality olive oil | 12–15 small cherry tomatoes | 2 rosemary sprigs | coarse sea salt

PREPARATION

Stir yeast into 250 ml/8.5 fl oz water. Mix flour and fine salt in a bowl (with a lid) and add the yeast water. Stir until smooth with a wooden spoon for 2–3 minutes. The dough should be rather soft and sticky. If not, add water by the tablespoon. Cover, place in the refrigerator, and let rise for at least 6 hours (but even 12 hours are ok). Take the bowl out of the refrigerator 1–2 hours before baking and let the mixture continue to rise at room temperature.

Preheat the oven to 230°C/445°F (convection oven 210°C/410°C). Brush a baking sheet with oil. Carefully remove the dough from the bowl with a scraper and let it flow evenly onto the baking sheet (the air chambers created during rising later give the focaccia crumb its characteristic appearance, which is why it's worthwhile handling the dough very gently indeed). Because of the soft dough consistency, the shape of the focaccia can only be influenced by how you pour it. However, this also goes well with the rustic character of the bread.

Dip your fingertips in the oil and press some distinct wells into the focaccia. Wash the tomatoes and press them into the dough at regular intervals. Generously sprinkle with oil so that some also collects in the wells. Wash the rosemary, shake dry, and finely chop. Distribute over the focaccia together with a little coarse sea salt. Bake in the oven on the second lowest rack for about 20 minutes until the focaccia is golden brown and crisp from both above and below. Take it out of the oven and cool on a wire rack.

CANTINETTA

CICERI E TRIA

A classic dish of the Italian *cucina povera* (poor-people's food), which is primarily at home on the Salentine Peninsula. "Just a noodle soup" at first glance, but what a soup! Homemade durum-wheat noodles completely without egg are not only boiled for it but one portion of them is also baked crisp in olive oil. Especially when the weather outside is gray and cold, a big bowl of Ciceri e Tria is my best pick-me-up.

INGREDIENTS

Soup for 4: 125 g/4.5 oz dried garbanzo beans (or 1 jar with a drained weight of 240 g/8.5 oz) | 1 onion | 1 garlic clove | 2 tbsp olive oil | 1.5 l/ 1.5 US quarts of vegetable or chicken broth | 2 bay leaves

Pasta for 4: 1/2 tsp fine sea salt | 150 g/5.25 oz durum-wheat flour (such as Semola di grano duro rimacinata 176 by De Cecco)

Plus: lots of olive oil | 1 garlic clove| 1 dried chili (optional) | freshly ground black pepper | Parmesan flakes (optional)

PREPARATION

Soak dried garbanzo beans overnight in plenty of cold water. Pour into a colander after at least 10 hours of soaking time and rinse with cold water.

For the pasta, dissolve salt in 75 ml/2.5 fl oz of very warm water. Place flour in a large bowl and add the saltwater by the tablespoon. Always work the liquid completely into the flour with your hands (crumble between your fingers) before adding the next tablespoon. With every minute that you knead the dough, which is not at all elastic at the start, it will become noticeably smoother. So be sure to knead it intensively for at least 5 minutes (if the dough is still much too dry, add a bit more water; if it's too sticky, add a bit more flour). Shape the dough into a ball, wrap in foil, and let rest for 30 minutes in the refrigerator.

For the soup, peel the onion and garlic. Dice finely and brown slightly in a large pot with oil over medium heat. Pour in the broth, add the drained garbanzo beans and bay leaves, cover and let everything simmer over a low heat for about 1 hour until the garbanzo beans are soft. (If you use the canned garbanzo beans, then you don't have to cook them until soft. The beans just have to be heated in the soup for a few minutes.)

Dust the pasta dough with a little flour and roll out thinly by hand or with the pasta machine (I go up to the setting 7 of 9). Cut into wide but short strips. Then spread out on a towel dusted with flour to dry.

Pour olive oil at least finger-thick into a large skillet and heat it with the peeled garlic clove and the chili. Fry one third of the pasta strands in several batches until golden brown and crisp (remove the chili and garlic before it becomes dark and bitter), and then drain on paper towels. Add the rest of the noodles to the soup and cook them al dente for 4–7 minutes, depending on the thickness of the noodles. Distribute soup on the plates. Add a bit of pepper and 1 squirt of olive oil, then garnish with the fried noodles. I also like to sprinkle some flakes of Parmesan on top.

preserves & presents

EARL GREY TUILES

"Ouch!" is the first word that comes to mind when I think about tuiles, and there's a reason for that: If you want to shape the very delicate wafers into small cups or even elegant little cones, then you have to do it as long as the baked cookie sheets are still hot. So there's a considerable danger of burning your fingers in the process. But, as is often the case, practice makes perfect. So don't get discouraged—whatever breaks tastes just as good as the shaped cookies! If you don't like Earl Grey, you can also use another type of black tea—or bake the recipe without any tea at all.

MAKES 4–5 COOKIE SHEETS
PREPARATION TIME: 25 MINUTES
PLUS 6–8 MINUTES OF BAKING PER COOKIE SHEET

- 50 g/1.75 oz clarified butter
- 50 g/1.75 oz flour
- 75 g/2.75 oz extra fine (caster) sugar
- 1/2 organic lemon
- 1 tsp Earl Grey tea leaves
- 2 medium egg whites
- 1 pinch fine sea salt

Plus

Silicon baking mat (you can use baking paper as a substitute)

Melt clarified butter over low heat in a small saucepan and let cool (cools more quickly if you pour it into another container). Preheat the oven to 200°C/390°F (convection oven 180°C/355°F).

Sift flour into a bowl and add the sugar. Wash the lemon in hot water, finely grate the zest (without the bitter white part) and add. Finely grind the Earl Grey tea leaves, sift into the flour, and mix everything until evenly distributed. Stir in the completely cooled clarified butter. Beat egg whites with salt until they are foamy but not yet stiff and mix into the dough. The result is a relatively tough dough.

Line the cookie sheet with the baking mat (in contrast to the baking paper, it doesn't slip when you spread the dough). Now spread the dough evenly and very thinly because it will brown at different times if you don't. The best way to do this is to use a brush or a soft silicon spatula. For tuiles or little cones, use your hands to spread the dough in small (about 10 cm/4 inch Ø) rounds. (If you want this to be very precise, place a round pastry cutter on the mat and brush the inside with dough). For little waffle cups that you can fill, the rounds must be one-and-a-half times as large. If this is too complicated for you, simply brush a rectangular shape on the baking mat (once again, equally thin). This can be cut into thin, decorative strips with a knife directly after baking. Whichever shape you decide on: Never put too much on a sheet at the same time because the dough must be shaped within a few seconds after baking.

Bake in the oven (middle rack) for 6–8 minutes until the dough has entirely turned a golden-brown color. Then take it out and remove the cookie sheets one by one with a spatula and shape quickly: For tuiles, simply place the round sheets over the handle of a cooking spoon; for little rolls, carefully wrap them around it. To make small cups, place them over the bottom of an upside-down glass or little bowl. Let cool completely. When stored in an airtight container, the cookies will stay crisp for several days. Classic with tea or ice cream.

WECK

PORK DRIPPING WITH APPLE

When friends from other countries visit us, they are always amazed at the Bavarian beer-garden culture and the tradition that allows people to bring along their own picnic basket: Under the shady chestnut trees, a checked tablecloth is spread out and a few freshly drawn liters of beer or Radler (beer mixed with lemonade) are picked up at the counter. A decent Bavarian Brotzeit (snack) includes Obatzda (cheese spread) and daikon radish, as well as chicken, pretzels, and crusty farmhouse bread. Plus pork dripping, which is best homemade with apple and onion. And please don't think about the calories—just enjoy it!

MAKES 3 JARS (EACH WITH A CAPACITY OF 200 ML/7 FL OZ)
PREPARATION TIME: 45 MINUTES PLUS TIME FOR COOLING

500 g/1.1 lb oz fat pork bacon (from the back)
1 onion
1 tart apple
Sea salt (fine)
Freshly ground black pepper

To Taste

Dried marjoram and thyme, bay leaves, finely chopped garlic

Plus

Canning or twist-off jars (sterilized)

Cut the pork bacon into cubes that aren't too small. Place in a large pot and render over medium heat, stirring occasionally. Caution: The more fat fries out of the bacon pieces, the more the whole thing will splatter. Even the crackling may occasionally jump out of the pot. Because of this, you should either put a spray guard over the pot or cover the pot with a lid and keep it open a crack.

In the meantime, peel the onion and chop into relatively fine cubes. Quarter, core, and peel the apple. Then cut each quarter in half and slice thinly crosswise. As soon as the crackling has turned a light golden-brown color (after 10–15 minutes), add the onion cubes and apple slices. Don't be startled if the mixture froths up intensely because it will settle down again fairly quickly. Season and taste (but be careful because it's very hot): I prefer just to season the dripping with salt and pepper, but obviously you can also add herbs or garlic.

Take the pot from the stove as soon as the onion and apple have also turned a golden color. Pour everything through a large sieve (set aside the fat) and distribute the crackling, onion, and apple between the jars. Fill up with the liquid fat, close the jars, and let cool. Together with crusty farmhouse bread, this makes a great snack. When stored in a cool place, the dripping will keep for several weeks.

Tip: If you intend to use the dripping soon, you can also simply fill it into little clay or pâté jars.

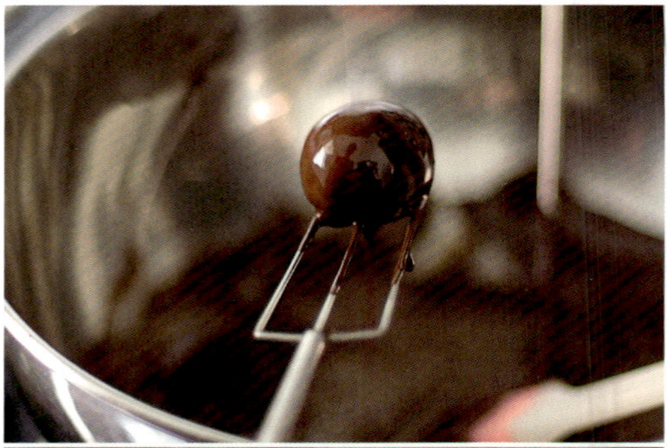

MOZART BALLS

This recipe comes from Sandra, my friend from school, who convinced me many years ago that homemade chocolates not only taste unbelievably good but are also astonishingly easy to make. Nowadays, whenever I can't decide on an appropriate gift, everyone always seems happy to receive the Mozart Balls with their pretty decoration. To present them as a gift, either stack them in a can lined with silk paper or fill them into little cellophane bags that can be tied with a colorful ribbon.

MAKES 36 PIECES
PREPARATION TIME: 1 HOUR
PLUS 30 MINUTES FOR COOLING AND TIME TO DRY

- 200 g/7 oz well-cooled nut nougat
- 3 tbsp pistachios (about 25 g/1 oz)
- 200 g/7 oz marzipan
- 80 g/3 oz icing sugar
- 1 tbsp Kirsch (cherry brandy or another type of fruit schnapps that you like)
- 150 g/5.25 oz milk or dark chocolate couverture (choose type according to your own taste)

Cut the nougat into 36 equal cubes. Quickly shape each cube into a ball (by pressing on them instead of rolling) so that the nougat doesn't get warm (it's a pretty smeary situation otherwise). Cover and place in the refrigerator for 30 minutes to harden.

Finely grind the pistachios in a mortar. Cut the marzipan into large cubes and place in a bowl. Sift the icing sugar over it and add two-thirds of the ground pistachios and the Kirsch. Use your hands to knead everything into an evenly blended mixture and then shape into 3–4 cm/1.25–1 .5 inch thick ropes on the work surface. Cut into 36 slices of equal size. Press each slice flat in your hand and place a nougat ball on it. Enclose the ball with the marzipan so that the nougat center is completely surrounded. Roll into balls between your hands. Place the finished balls back in the refrigerator covered until you are ready to work with them again.

Line a cookie sheet with baking paper. Temper the chocolate: Finely chop the chocolate coating, place two thirds of it in a metal bowl, and slowly let it melt over a hot bain-marie while stirring (the chocolate will get lumpy if it becomes too hot in the process). When you do this, do not let the bowl touch the water or allow water to get into the chocolate coating. Once the chocolate coating has melted completely, take the bowl out of the bain-marie and stir in the rest of the chopped chocolate coating until it has also melted.

With a (truffle) fork, dip each ball into the chocolate coating one by one, let drip briefly, and carefully place on the sheet. Sprinkle with the rest of the ground pistachios and let dry in a cool room. Then pack airtight in jars and store in a cool place. The Mozart Balls will keep for several weeks like this, but they taste best fresh.

HOMEMADE LEMONADE

was always something special for us children, even if the recipe from my grandmother consisted of nothing more than water, lemon juice, and sugar. Filled to the top with ice cubes and lemon slices, the pitcher was always emptied within the shortest time. Even today, I still can't get enough of it on hot summer days. My three favorite variations offer the right beverage for every taste.

MAKES 700 ML/24 FL OZ OF SYRUP EACH
PREPARATION TIME: 20–30 MINUTES PER SYRUP
PLUS TIME FOR STEEPING AND COOLING

Lime-Basil Syrup
- 4–5 limes (2 of them organic)
- 300 g/10.5 oz sugar
- 1 bunch of basil

Ginger-Iced Tea Syrup
- 3–4 lemons (1 of them organic)
- 1 piece of fresh ginger (2–3 cm/about 1 inch)
- 300 g/10.5 oz sugar
- 3 tsp Earl Grey tea leaves
- Tea sieve or tea-paper filter

Red Berry Syrup
- 500 g/1.1 lb fresh or frozen mixed red berries (such as blueberries, strawberries, raspberries, red currants, blackberries and cherries)
- 1/2 lemon
- 300 g/10.5 oz sugar

Plus
- Bottles that seal well (sterilized)

Lime-Basil Syrup—tart & fresh
Wash the organic limes with hot water and finely grate the zest. Squeeze out the juice of all the limes, which should yield 150 ml/5 fl oz. Boil 350 ml/12 fl oz water, sugar, and lime zest and juice in a pot and let simmer for 5 minutes over low heat. Remove from the stove. Tear the basil leaves into coarse pieces and stir into the citrus syrup. Let steep and take on the aroma for about 1 hour. Then pour through a fine sieve and squeeze the basil well with a spoon. Fill the syrup into the sterilized bottles and seal well. Or use the syrup immediately after several hours of cooling time.

Ginger-Iced Tea Syrup—spicy & tart (my favorite)
Wash the organic lemon with hot water and finely grate the zest. Squeeze out the juice of all the lemons, which should yield 150 ml/5 fl oz. Wash the ginger and finely grate or chop with the peel. Boil everything with 350 ml/12 fl oz water and sugar in a pot, and then take from the stove. Fill the tea leaves into the sieve or filter and add to the syrup. Let steep and take on the aroma for 5 minutes. Then slightly squeeze the tea leaves and remove. Pour the syrup through a fine sieve, fill into the sterilized bottles, and seal well. Or use the syrup immediately after several hours of cooling time.

Red Berry Syrup—fruity & sweet
You can use the frozen fruit as it is without first defrosting it. Pick over the fresh fruit, wash if necessary, clean, and remove the stones or strip off the stalks. Squeeze the lemon. Place the fruit and lemon juice in a pot with 300 ml/10 fl oz water and the sugar, bring to a boil, and let simmer over a low heat for 5 minutes. Pour the entire contents of the pot through a large sieve while carefully squeezing the fruit with a ladle. Fill the syrup into sterilized bottles and seal well. Or use the syrup immediately after several hours of cooling time.

Use
Dilute the syrup with water or sparkling mineral water in a ratio of 1:3 or 1:4 and serve with ice cubes. A shot of Red Berry Syrup turns Prosecco or Martini bianco into a colorful aperitif. The syrup keeps for a few days when stored in the refrigerator.

BLOOD-ORANGE JELLY WITH THYME

My grandparents' cellar and adjoining laundry room were always a true land of milk and honey: Next to two gigantic freezers—one of them with a lid so heavy that I couldn't even open it as a child—and a rickety wooden rack that had fresh fruit and vegetables concealed behind its dreadful 1970s curtain, there was primarily an abundance of one thing: preserves. Even though you could also find one or more jars with pickled vegetables or fruit in alcohol, several dozen preserving jars with sweet marmalades and jellies dominated the scene. Strawberry jam, raspberry jam, cherry jam, currant jelly, elder jelly with apple and plum jelly were part of the standard repertoire. Without exception, they were all made from the fruit from their own garden and supplies never seemed to run out.

Although I never make jams and jellies in the amounts that my grandparents produced back then, this has still remained a cherished tradition. And they taste so much better than what you can buy at the store!

MAKES 5–6 JARS (WITH A CAPACITY OF 200 ML/7 FL OZ EACH)
PREPARATION TIME: 30 MINUTES

- 8–10 sprigs of thyme
- 1 vanilla pod
- 2–3 kg/4.4–6.6 lbs blood oranges (depending on their juice content, I like to add 1 lemon and 2 pink grapefruits to them)
- 1 kg/2.2 lb preserving sugar (1:1) or 500 g/1.1 lb preserving sugar (1:2)

Plus

- Kitchen yarn
- Twist-off jars (sterilized)

Wash the thyme and shake it dry, then bind with the kitchen yarn into a little bouquet. Slice open the vanilla pod lengthwise and scrape out the pulp. Squeeze the oranges (and the grapefruits and lemon if used), pour the juice through a fine sieve, and measure off 1 l/1 US quart. Put into a large pot together with the preserving sugar, thyme, and vanilla pod with its pulp. Stir well and bring to a boil. Then keep it at a rolling boil over medium to high heat for 5 minutes and stir occasionally. Do a jelling test before the end of the cooking time: Put a few drops of juice on a plate. If these turn into a solid jelly within a few seconds, then you can fill the juice into the jars. Otherwise, extend the cooking time by 1–2 more minutes. Remove the thyme and the pod.

Fill the juice into the jars to just below the top (use a funnel to avoid spills) and close tightly. It's best to use a dish towel because the jars are very hot! Whether or not you turn the filled jars upside down for a few minutes (to kill the germs in the remaining air) is a matter of faith. Then turn them right side up to let them cool off completely. Now check to see whether a vacuum has formed—the lid no longer "clicks" when you press on it. Perfect! Stored in a cool and dark place, the jelly will keep for up to 1 year in the closed jars. And if a vacuum really hasn't developed, then just eat the jelly right at your next breakfast.

Tip: If you don't want to use preserving sugar, you can also make the jelly with regular sugar and add citric acid or pectin (from the pharmacy or even from well-stocked supermarkets). In this case, adjust the ratios of the amounts and the cooking time according to the manufacturer's recommendation.

CHICKEN-LIVER-PORCINI PÂTÉ WITH PISTACHIOS

"I eat everything, just not innards!" is what I hear on a regular basis when I ask my guests about their eating habits. But it actually just depends on how you prepare them. In any case, no one has been able to say no to this creamy pâté with porcinis and Marsala. The pistachios give it the special crunch effect. Try it and enjoy it. Or give it as a present and make someone happy.

SERVES 4–6
(OR 1 FORM WITH A CAPACITY OF ABOUT 350 ML/12 FL OZ)
PREPARATION TIME: 30 MINUTES PLUS 2 HOURS FOR COOLING

- 5 g/0.2 oz dried porcinis
- 200 g/7 oz chicken livers
- 75 g/2.75 oz butter
- 3–4 thyme sprigs
- 1 scallion
- Sea salt (fine)
- Freshly ground black pepper
- 2 tbsp Marsala
- 2 tbsp Crème Double
- 2–3 tbsp salted pistachio nuts
- 3 tbsp duck fat (or butter as a substitute)

Soak porcinis in hot water for at least 15 minutes, then squeeze the water out of them and finely chop. In the meantime, wash the chicken livers under running cold water and let drain on paper towels. Remove the sinews and membrane. Cut large livers in half. Melt 50 g/1.75 oz of the butter in a small saucepan and let cool.

Wash the thyme and shake dry, then pluck off the little leaves. Peel the scallion and dice finely. Let the rest of the butter foam in a pan over medium heat and brown the scallion in it until translucent. Add the thyme, as well as the prepared livers and the porcinis. Sear the livers on all sides (for a total time of about 6 minutes, test by cutting one of the thicker pieces, which should hardly be pink inside by now). Salt and pepper, pour in the Marsala.

The entire contents of the pan should be pureed, but not too finely, in an electric grinder. Then mix in the cooled butter and Crème Double. Coarsely chop the pistachios and mix about half into the pâté. Fill the pâté into a porcelain form, cover, and chill for 1 hour in the refrigerator.

Melt the duck fat over low heat and spread over the pâté with a tablespoon. Evenly distribute the rest of the pistachios over it and cool the pâté again for at least 1 hour. If you cover it well, it will keep in the refrigerator for several days. It's best served with bread fresh from the oven.

BUTTER CARAMELS WITH FLEUR DE SEL

Just so I don't get any complaints afterward: The combination of sweet butter caramel and delicate salt crystals should simply be prohibited—you'll get hooked on these caramels! Although it does take some practice at the beginning to not let the caramel burn and to take it from the stove at exactly the right time, the effort is worth it and gets easier with every attempt. Even if my dentist wouldn't be very enthusiastic about them...

MAKES ABOUT 50 PIECES
PREPARATION TIME: 30 MINUTES
PLUS 1–2 HOURS FOR HARDENING

A few drops of sunflower oil
75 g/2.75 oz butter
200 g/7 oz cream
75 g/2.75 oz golden syrup (English sugar syrup that is available at well-stocked supermarkets)
200 g/7 oz sugar
1/2 tsp Fleur de Sel/Maldon sea salt (plus a bit more for the finish)

Plus

Candy thermometer
Wax paper for wrapping

Line a shallow, square form (about 14 x 14 cm/5.5 x 5.5 inches) with baking paper and lightly grease it with oil. Bring butter and cream to a boil in a small saucepan, then keep warm.

Put the 75 ml/ 2.5 fl oz water, golden syrup, and sugar in a large saucepan over medium to high heat and stir until the sugar has dissolved. Let the mixture simmer until it turns golden-yellow and reaches a temperature of 115°C/240°F (measure with a candy thermometer). Then stir in the butter cream, which will cause the mixture to foam up vigorously briefly. Let simmer for 10–15 minutes while stirring continuously until the caramel has reached a temperature of about 120°C/250°F (for soft caramels) or 125°C/260°F (for harder caramels). Take from the stove and stir in the salt. Pour the caramel mixture into the prepared form and let cool and harden for 1–2 hours.

Then flip the butter caramel over onto a board and pull off the baking paper. Cut the caramel into longish rectangles and—this works only for soft caramels—press a bit of Fleur de Sel into the surface for the finish so that some of the salt crystals stick to it. Creates a sensational taste experience!

Either store the butter caramels in an airtight, closed jar (place a piece of baking paper between each layer in this case) or wrap the individual pieces in wax paper.

Tea-Vanilla Caramels: Prepare the caramels as above but steep 1 vanilla pod that has been sliced open lengthwise, together with its pulp, and 1–2 tea bags (such as Earl Grey, Chai) for 5–10 minutes in the hot butter cream (then remove the pod and bags). Leave out the salt.

Cocoa Caramels: Prepare the caramels as above but stir in 1–2 tbsp of unsweetened cocoa powder just before the caramel reaches the desired temperature (120°C/250°F or 125°C/260°F). Leave out the salt.

ROASTED ALMONDS

are part of every visit to a public festival or Christmas fair in Germany: Even from far away, the aroma of the caramelized nuts gets into your nostrils. Before you know it, you are already holding one of the colorfully printed little bags in your hands, nibbling with relish down to the last almond. But that was before I learned how easy it is to make these munchies in my own kitchen. You will need a bit of patience during the caramelizing and should be careful in handling the hot sugar, but otherwise: child's play. Be sure to try it out, and you can even use other nuts as a variation!

ENOUGH FOR 4–6 AS A SNACK
PREPARATION TIME: 20 MINUTES

125 g/4.5 oz sugar
2 tbsp vanilla sugar
1/2–1 tsp powdered cinnamon
200 g/7 oz almonds with skin (other good choices are walnuts, macadamia nuts, hazelnuts, pecans...)

Line a cookie sheet with baking paper.

Boil 100 ml/3.5 fl oz water, sugar, vanilla sugar, and cinnamon in a large saucepan. Then add the almonds and let everything cook over medium to high heat while stirring occasionally. After 5–8 minutes, the liquid will have evaporated and the sugar covers the almonds with a dry crust.

Now reduce the temperature somewhat and keep stirring until the sugar turns liquid again and coats all of the almonds evenly as caramel. Shake onto the prepared cookie sheet. Quickly separate the almonds from each other with two forks (not with your fingers because they are very hot!) and then let them cool. The almonds keep for several days in an airtight container, but taste best when they are very fresh and still slightly warm.

Chili Walnuts: If you like things a bit spicier, you can try the following variation: Instead of the cinnamon powder, simply add 1/4 – 1/2 tsp chili flakes and 1/2 tsp medium-hot, smoked paprika powder (Pimentón de la Vera); instead of the almonds, use walnuts here. Plus: When the sugar becomes liquid again, sprinkle a bit of Fleur de Sel on the nuts.

I believe, no—I know—that I have never worked on a project that has been as demanding in so many different ways as this book—including the ecstatic leaps for joy and the desperate hair-pulling. It accompanied me at every turn for an entire year and I grew fonder of it every day.

A HUGE THANK-YOU TO...

...my publishing company Gräfe und Unzer, especially Georg Kessler, Doris Birk, and Birgit Rademacker, who courageously agreed to my concept and allowed me creative freedom in the right places.

...my editor Sabine Sälzer, who accompanied me right from the start with her enormous wealth of experience and her unbelievable capacity for enthusiasm. This book would not exist without her.

...my copy editor Christina Kempe, whose heartwarming laughter always cheered me up and motivated me, even when the deadlines were tight. Together with Sabine, this is the best team that a fledgling book author could wish for.

...Sebastian Dickhaut, best-selling cookbook author and good friend, who I especially value because of his big heart and boundless curiosity about life. He set the ball rolling.

...the readers of deliciousdays.com and all food bloggers: The culinary side of the internet was the greatest enrichment of recent years for me. It has never been easier to immerse yourself in other people's kitchens, discover new dishes and ingredients, and exchange ideas with food aficionadas from all over the world.

...all of the dear friends, colleagues, test eaters and test cooks who never got tired of helping me with their feedback and contributing ideas, especially Coco Lang, Kristin Hellmig, Harry Baeck, Franzi Brauner, Maria Baier, Hande and Theo Leimer, Stephanie and David Kunstle (& family), the Dickerson family, Emily Nyquist, Sherry and Bob Page, Georg Haury, Erika Bürk, Ulrike Sepp, Katrin Eymers, Sven Lehmann, Sabine Schöfer, Hans Hollweck, Ulli Hauser, Birgit Krennbauer, Mauro Mahjoub, Ruth Idris, Eddie Ibrahim, Dagmar and Craig Davis, Anja Weisbach, Carlos Martinez, Saskia Turner, Kevin Scoones, Sylvie Obers, Stefan Birkel, Carol Andrej Stockinger, Juan Vazquez Regueiro, Patricia Holler, Elise Bauer, Josh Friedman, David Lebovitz, Johanna Wagner, Petra Holzapfel, Kelli Bernard, Beate Muschler, Maike Damm, Tanja Dusy, Bettina Matthaei, Bärbel and Wolf Seidel, Ruth and Rudi Herfurtner, Mathilde Strasser, Fritz Weich, Lena and Gitti Henneberg, Joachim Fischer, and the Kaltmamsell.

...my family, who gave me the loving of cooking and good food and their endless patience until I could make friends with green vegetables, mushrooms, and all kinds of other things. Grandma Luise for my most beautiful childhood memories in her kitchen.

...Oliver. For simply everything.

PRACTICAL INFORMATION

Although I consciously wrote deliciousdays.com in English from the start because I thought it was especially fascinating to communicate with people from other countries and cultures who are enthusiastic about cooking, this internationality also involved some hurdles. I was used to measuring my ingredients (especially when baking) with a digital scale in grams, but many American readers prefer to measure according to volume using measuring spoons (cups and spoons) while others use measuring units such as ounces (OZ) or measure the oven temperatures according to Fahrenheit (°F) instead of Celsius (°C).

Those who like to look beyond the rim of their own plates into foreign pots and try out recipes from other countries are best equipped with some basic tools: Anyone can afford a digital kitchen scale that permits switching from grams to ounces, as well as a cup-and-spoon set. In addition, a small, separate oven thermometer with a Celsius and Fahrenheit display not only prevents the annoyance of converting, but also serves to monitor the actual temperature in the oven.

Wheat flour: Since the types of German wheat flour are not common in all countries, the following rule of thumb can be used for recipes in this book (you may have to slightly adapt the amounts you use until the dough has reached the desired consistency):
Type 405: Flour for finer pastry (such as unbleached pastry flour)
Type 550: Flour for more rustic pastry and bread (such as unbleached all-purpose flour/unbleached bread flour)

Yeast: I prefer to bake with fresh yeast and highly recommend it, even if you have to spend extra time searching for it in some countries (either on the milk shelves of supermarkets or ask at the little bakery on the corner). If you still want to work with dry yeast or have no choice, then use about half the weight of the fresh yeast or follow the recommendations on the yeast package that you are using. The great thing about baking with yeast is that a few grams more or less have little effect on the results of the baking—when in doubt, the dough needs just a bit more (or less) time to rise beautifully.

Conversion Information (rounded off)

According to Volume:

Milliliters (Metric) =	Fluid OZ (Imperial) =	Fluid OZ (US) =	Tablespoon (US) =	Cup (US)
30 ml	1.05 fl oz	1 fl oz	2 TBSP	1/8
60 ml	2.1 fl oz	2 fl oz	4 TBSP	1/4
80 ml	2.8 fl oz	2.7 fl oz	5.3 TBSP	1/3
120 ml	4.2 fl oz	4 fl oz	8 TBSP	1/2
240 ml	8.4 fl oz	8.1 fl oz	16 TBSP	1

1 TSP = 5 ml
1 TBSP = 15 ml
1 US quart = 1 l = 1000 ml

According to Weight:

1 ounce	=	30 g
1 pound	=	450 g
100 g	=	3.5 oz

Celcius	=	Fahrenheit
100 °C	=	210 °F
120 °C	=	250 °F
140 °C	=	285 °F
160 °C	=	320 °F
180 °C	=	355 °F
200 °C	=	390 °F
220 °C	=	430 °F
230 °C	=	445 °F

Further assistance in converting various measuring units can be found online:

http://unit-converter.org
http://www.gourmetsleuth.com/conversions.htm
http://www.metric-conversions.org/

INDEX

So you can find recipes with certain ingredients even more quickly, this index additionally has popular ingredients such as **eggs** or **herbs**—also arranged alphabetically and in bold—above the respective recipes.

IMPRINT

Nicole Stich Her incomparable passion for cooking and travelling is what inspired Nicole Stich to create www.deliciousdays.com at the beginning of 2005: The internationally renowned food blog offers a successful mix of her own recipes and anecdotes, food news, and stylish food photography. In addition to giving Nicole Stich a large readership and numerous awards, it has also changed her professional life. Because of her passion for eating, writing, and photographing, she put her career as a designer on hold and authored her first cookbook for Gräfe und Unzer – a colorful combination of irresistible recipes, personal experiences, and pictures that whet your appetite.

Doris Birk:
Program Manager

Birgit Rademacker:
Editor-in-Chief

Sabine Sälzer:
Project Manager, Editorial Department

Nicole Stich:
Design & layout, cover design, photos

Redaktionsbüro Christina Kempe, Munich: Editing German edition; typesetting/DTP/design

independent medien design:
Art direction

bookwise Medienproduktion GmbH, Munich
Coordination of English edition

Christine M. Grimm:
Translation

Jane Michael:
Proof Reading

Markus Plötz:
Production

Longo AG, Bolzano:
Color separation

Firmengruppe APPL, Wemding:
Printing and binding

Picture credits

Nicole Stich: all photos except…

Oliver Seidel: pp. 7, 15, 19, 26, 36, 41 top right, 42, 45 top right, 50, 71 top left and bottom left, 73 step fotos, 127 bottom left and top right, 128 bottom left, 130, 139, 150 top right and bottom left, 154 top right, 165, 176 bottom left, 177, 184, 188, 204/5, 215

The Völkl family (private): pp. 94, 97, 98, 100

Cadicamo Photography: p. 73 top right

ISBN 978-3-8338-1538-6

1st Edition 2008

GRÄFE UND UNZER

Ein Unternehmen der
GANSKE VERLAGSGRUPPE

Our Guarantee

All of the information in this guide has been carefully and conscientiously checked. However, if it should happen to contain an error, send the book with the corresponding reference to our Reader Service. We will exchange the GU guide for another book on the same or a similar topic.

Dear Reader,

We are pleased that you have decided on a GU book. With your purchase, you are relying on the quality, competence, and up-to-dated status of our guides. We thank you for this! We want to become even better as the leading guide publishing company. This is why your opinion is so important to us. Please send us your suggestions, your criticism, or your praise for our books. Do you have questions or require further advice on a topic? We look forward to hearing from you!

We are here for you!
Monday–Thursday:
8:00 a.m. – 6:00 p.m.;
Friday: 8:00 a.m. – 4:00 p.m.
Tel.: +49-0180-5005054*
Fax: +49- 0180-5012054*
E-mail:
leserservice@graefe-und-unzer.de

P.S.: If you want to have even more up-to-date information from GU, you can subscribe to our free GU Online Newsletter and/or our free customer magazine.

GRÄFE UND UNZER VERLAG
Reader Service
Postfach 86 03 13
81630 München

*(0,14 €/min. from the German landline network/ mobile phones-price may deviate)

"The purpose of a cookery book is one and unmistakable. Its object can conceivably be no other than to increase the happiness of mankind."

Joseph Conrad